Junior | GIRL SCOUT®

HANDBOOK

Girl Scouts of the USA | 420 Fifth Avenue | New York, NY 10018

National President
Connie L. Matsui

National Executive Director
Marsha Johnson Evans

National Director, Membership, Program and Diversity
Sharon Woods Hussey

Director, Program Development
Harriet S. Mosatche, Ph.D.

Project Directors
Harriet S. Mosatche, Ph.D.
Karen Unger

Authors
Chris Bergerson, María Cabán, Rosemarie Cryan, Dee Ebersole-Boukouzis, Toni Eubanks, Sharon Hussey, Carolyn Kennedy, Harriet S. Mosatche, Ph. D, Karen Unger

Contributors
Melissa Algranati, Sheila K. Lewis, Margarita Magner, Alexandra O' Rourke

Acknowledgements
Director of Publishing, Suzanna Penn; Project Editor, Mikki Morrissette; Assistant Editor, Susan Brody; Manager, Creative Design and Production, Christina Cannard-Seward

Illustration
Adam Hurwitz: 5, 9, 45, 51, 74-75, 83, 89, 107, 114, 122, 134m, r, 138-139, 146-149, 155r, m, 160, 162-163, 173tr, 176, 181, 184-185; Sara Schwartz: 41, 44, 46-47, 49-50, 78-79, 84, 98-99, 127, 136, 165, 170; Karen Stormer Brooks: 7, 29, 36-37, 52-55, 69, 73, 86, 105r, 135, 140-141, 155l, 156-159, 174, 179; William Waitzman: 22, 35, 59l, r-60, 63, 65, 77, 87-88, 91-92, 94, 103, 105l, 106, 108-109, 169, 173tl, c, 177

Photography
The Girl Scout Archives: III, 2, 4, 9; The Girl Scouts: Lori Adamski-Peek Cover, III, IV, V, 2, 3, 6, 10, 11, 12,16,17, 20, 21, 31, 40, 41,42, 58, 66, 76, 104, 105m, 110, 111, 128, 145, 149,154,187, 188, 189l, 202; Elizabeth Hathon V, 172; George Kerrigan/Digital Eyes: all badges, awards, insignia; 15, 21,28,61, 76,80,128, 132, 133, 161, 166, 167 Babs Armour 59, 61; Corbis: Owen Franken 74, Hughes Martin 61, Roger Reesemeyer143, Richard Hamilton Smith 61; Joseph De Sciose 20, 21, 31; Envison Steven Needham 58, 68,118, 120,121, Amy Reichman 129r,135,137; FPG John Lawlor 62, Bob Peterson 77, 89, Arthur Tilley 172, 186, VCG 180; Ken Karp 15, 129m, 134; Mountain Stock: Hank de Vre 110, Omni-Photo: Esbin/Anderson 076, Jeff Greenberg 125; Peter Arnold, Inc.: Jodi Jacobson 175, Ray Pfortner 128, 150; PhotoEdit: Michelle Bridwell 186, Myrleen Cate 51, 126, Richard Hutchings 154, Felicia Martinez 173, 178, Michael Newman 50, Nancy Sheehan 58, 66,186, Frank Siteman 41, 56, David Young-wolff 20, 38, 49, 61, 104, 124, 155, 164l; Photo Researchers: Grantpix 154, 164r, David M. Grossman 48, Ken Lax 74, Jeff Lepore 120, Will & Demi McIntyre 121, Rod Plank 118, 119, Blair Seitz 126; Stock Options:Bachmann 58; Stone: Charles Gupton 187; The Image works: Bob Daemmrich 43, 51, 61,104, 113, Jeff Greenberg 58, 61, James Marshall 31; The Stock Market: Arthur Beck 119, Peter Beck 142, DiMaggio/Klish 112, John Henley 64, Ted Horowitz 40, 50, LWA-Dann Tardif 057, Ariel Skelley 41, 43, Tom Stewart 186, Jon P. Yeager 172

Design
Adventure House, NYC

Inquiries related to the *Junior Girl Scout Handbook* should be directed to
Membership, Program and Diversity,
Girl Scouts of the USA, 420 Fifth Avenue, New York, N.Y. 10018-2798.

"The Food Guide Pyramid" on page 114, is provided courtesy of the U.S. Department of Agriculture.

First Impression 2001
Printed in the United States of America
ISBN 0-88441-619-4

10 9 8 7 6

Junior GIRL SCOUT® HANDBOOK

CONTENTS

1 *Girl Scout Basics*

Do you want to know more about how you fit into the world's largest organization for girls? Learn all about Girl Scouting in this chapter.

2 *Adventures in Girl Scouting*

Try out your leadership skills by managing money, planning trips, and doing service projects.

3 It's Great to Be a Girl

Find out about the power of being a girl in this chapter.

4 Family and Friends

Learn how to have fun with family and friends.

5 How to Stay Safe

Learn how to keep yourself and others safe.

6 Be Healthy, Be Fit

Discover how to keep fit, eat right, cut stress, and manage your time better.

7 Let's Get Outdoors

Explore the wonderful world of the outdoors, both near and far.

8 Create and Invent

Use your imagination to create and invent something just for you.

9 Explore and Discover

Find out the why's of how things work.

10 Junior Girl Scout Awards

Discover the special awards you can earn as a Junior Girl Scout.

Welcome to GIRL

CONGRATULATIONS ON BECOMING A JUNIOR GIRL SCOUT!

Whether you've just joined or you've bridged from Brownie Girl Scouts, you're about to enter a world of fun, friends, and adventures.

As a Junior Girl Scout, you can do the activities in this book—your *Junior Girl Scout Handbook*—as well as earn the badges in the *Junior Girl Scout Badge Book*. You can do activities online at the Girl Scout Web site, www.girlscouts.org in the "Just for Girls" section. And there are lots of other resources on special topics: *Issues for Girl Scouts* books, *Fun and Easy Nature and Science Investigations*, *Girl Scouts Go Global*, *GirlSports* books, and more.

SCOUTS

What's Inside?

Your handbook is the basic tool for Junior Girl Scouts. It contains all the information you need to know about being a Junior Girl Scout. Each chapter is filled with activities for you to do with other Girl Scouts, with friends and family, or by yourself. You can do these activities in or outside of Girl Scout meetings.

What To Do With It

The activities in this handbook are based on the Girl Scout Promise and Law. By doing these activities, you learn more about what it means to be a Girl Scout. Girls all across the United States and in USA Girl Scouts Overseas troops are doing activities from this very same handbook.

Since Junior Girl Scouts may be in third, fourth, fifth, or sixth grade, you might find some activities to be a bit harder than others, or some activities that are too easy. You don't have to do everything in the book. You and your friends can pick what you feel will be possible and, most importantly, fun and interesting. You can always ask your leader or another adult to help you modify an activity that seems too difficult for you.

You will find that activities that contain measurements are footnoted. You can turn to the chart on page 208 of this book to discover how to convert these measurements into the metric system.

You may write in your handbook, take notes, draw pictures, or attach things to the pages. You don't have to read the chapters in any order, though you might want to start with Chapter One. Your Girl Scout leader can help you decide what to do next. She can also help you find the resources you might need to complete your activities.

Alphabetical Index

You will find an index at the end of the book. An index is an alphabetical listing of topics you can find in the book. For instance, if you are interested in finding information about "ceremonies" or "first aid" quickly, just look these topics up in the index and you will find the page(s) where they are mentioned.

1 Girl Scout Basics

In This Chapter You Will Learn About:

Since 1912, Girl Scouts just like you have had fun making new friends, trying new activities, and helping in their communities.

How Girl Scouting Began

One woman—Juliette Gordon Low—or Daisy (her nickname)—had a dream for girls in the United States. She wanted girls to grow strong, feel successful, support each other, and become accomplished at doing things that girls didn't ordinarily do. She herself was an amazing woman—strong, determined, open to new ideas, and never stopped by her hearing disability. Here, she can tell you herself:

Most of you may know me as the founder of Girl Scouts of the USA. But I imagine very few of you know about me as a girl your age. I'm sure I wasn't much different from many of you.

A Letter from Daisy Low

I attended boarding school in New York City, and the letter below is one of hundreds I wrote throughout my life. In fact, before telephones and e-mail, letter writing was how people kept in touch.

My darling Mama,
I rise at six, study an hour before breakfast which is at eight. During the morning I have nothing but French studies. At twelve we have lunch. Three times a week I go to my drawing. I wish you could see my teacher. He is a perfect character. On Saturday morning I go with five other girls from here to Dodsworth's dancing school where they are so swell, but I like it and know already lots of people there.

Daisy

More About Daisy Low

My full name is Juliette Magill Kinzie Gordon Low. I was born on October 31, 1860, a few months before the Civil War began. My birthday fell on Halloween.

When my father wrote to his family in Chicago about me, one of my uncles exclaimed, "I'll bet she'll be a daisy!" And I remained "Daisy" to my family and to many of my close friends all my life.

I was part of a large family who played and had fun together. I loved animals of all kinds, and had some pretty unusual ones. My pet parrot and mockingbird were two of my favorites.

Drawing was my favorite subject in school, and I was good at learning foreign languages. But spelling and arithmetic gave me problems. At times I was too active and fun-loving to sit still in school. My mother wrote: "I send a list of your words (spelled) wrong and the right way to spell them. Please study them hard, as you frequently, in fact, always, spell them wrongly."

Daisy's Spelling	Right Way
sleave	sleeve
idear	idea
disgrase	disgrace
suspence	suspense

On December 21, 1886, when I was 26 years old, I married an Englishman named Willy Low. I had already lost some hearing in one of my ears. As I was leaving the ceremony, a piece of rice landed in my good ear and the doctor who removed the grain of rice punctured my eardrum. Eventually, I became almost totally deaf, but that didn't stop me from what I was going to do next.

Etowah Cliffs
November 8, 1876

Oh Mama!
I feel perfectly miserable, because you're going to give me an awful scolding and I know I deserve it. I've lost my beautiful little ring with the blue forget-me-nots on it that Uncle Julian sent from Europe to me!!!
This is the way I lost it. Percy lent me his gold pencil to wear around my neck on a ribbon, and I lent him my ring (I know you will say "the little fool" but I expect you lent your rings to boys when you were a girl) and of course I didn't know he would lose it, but he did and he felt awfully about it. . . .
Your prodigal daughter,

Daisy

How Girl Scouting Came to the U.S.A

I was 52 years old when I made the long boat trip home from England. I couldn't wait to get home because I was bringing exciting news to share with girls all over the United States.

Girl Scouts playing basketball in about 1912.

Daisy Low

A team of Girl Scouts basketball players in 1912.

I was good friends with Lord Baden-Powell, who founded the Boy Scouts, and his sister Agnes. She was helping girls form their own group called Girl Guides. Lord Baden-Powell told me that "there are little stars that guide us on, although we do not realize it." I thought about this saying while I was deciding what I should do next in life, and the direction seemed clear: start Girl Scouts in the United States.

In the United States, I started the first Girl Scout troop in 1912 with my niece, who was also named Daisy Gordon. She was the first Girl Scout in the United States. The first Girl Scouts played sports—just like you do today! Daisy Gordon loved to play basketball. In 1912, girls wore enormous pleated gymnasium bloomers to play basketball. They had to cover themselves with overcoats that reached their ankles to cross the street to get to the basketball lot. Before taking off their overcoats, they pulled together huge canvas curtains strung on wires that surrounded the basketball field. That way, nobody could see their bloomered legs from the street!

Girl Scout Traditions Continue

Today, Girl Scouts continue many of the same traditions and activities they did when there were only 3,000 Girl Scouts in 1916. You can read more about what Girl Scouts did in 1916 in the first Girl Scout historical novel, *Octavia's Girl Scout Journey: Savannah 1916*, and on the Girl Scout Web site, or try making a Girl Scout scrapbook (see the next page).

Today there are over three million Girl Scouts from all parts of the United States. There are many more Girl Scouts or Girl Guides in over 100 countries around the world. What do Girl Scouts and Girl Guides around the world have in common? They each honor the same three basic parts of the Girl Scout Promise that guide their values. They work on projects, help other people, and become leaders in their communities. They plan many trips and activities that are different from what they might usually do. Most importantly, Girl Scouts and Girl Guides learn how to work with and support each other, and have a great time.

Activity:

A Girl Scout Scrapbook

The word "scrapbook" came from the fact that people in the Victorian era, like Daisy, loved to collect "scrap," which were special invitations, programs, postcards, menus, advertisements, calling cards, letters, magazine illustrations, locks of hair, dried flowers, photographs, and other souvenirs.

You can decorate the cover of your scrapbook the way girls in Daisy's time did, with lace and flowers, or embroidered fabric. Or, you can design a contemporary scrapbook. Arts and crafts and hobby stores sell scrapbook materials and kits. You can also find Web sites with scrapbook-making ideas.

What You Do

1. Use heavy paper or cardboard for the covers.
2. Use firm blank paper for your pages.
3. Line up the cover and inside pages.
4. Punch two holes through the covers and pages.
5. Tie them all together with ribbon or twine.

Now you can put your collectibles and keepsakes on the pages.

Dear Sarah,
I had so much fun last summer when we went to the beach. You are a terrific swimmer! Let's go to the same beach again next summer. Then you can teach me the crawl and butterfly stroke.
Your best friend
Lydia

Ice Skating
Extravaganza

Women's Basketball League
BASKETBALL TOUR
3:00 PM

Being a Junior Girl Scout

The Girl Scout Promise and Law are the basics of Girl Scouting. All Girl Scouts say them. All Girl Scouts try to live them. The activities you do in Girl Scouting are based on them.

For example, when you plan a service project you are helping others. When you clean up your campsite, you are keeping your country clean and protecting the environment for others to enjoy. When you learn about managing your money or giving first aid or planning a trip, you are learning to be a responsible and capable person.

The Girl Scout PROMISE

On my honor, I will try:
To serve God and my country,
To help people at all times,
And to live by the Girl Scout Law.

Promesa de las Girl Scouts

Por mi honor, yo trataré:
De servir a Dios, y a mi patria,
Ayudar a las personas en todo momento,
Y vivir conforme a la Ley de las Girl Scouts.

The Girl Scout LAW

I will do my best to be:
Honest and fair,
Friendly and helpful,
Considerate and caring,
***Courageous** and **strong**, and*
Responsible for what I say and do,
And to
respect myself and others,
respect authority,
use resources wisely,
***make the world a better place**, and*
be a sister to every Girl Scout.

La Ley de las Girl Scouts

Yo me esforzaré a:
Ser honrada y justa,
Cordial y servicial,
Considerada y compasiva,
Valiente y fuerte, y
Responsable de lo que digo y hago,
Y a respetarme a mi misma y a los demás,
Respetar la autoridad,
Usar los recursos de manera prudente,
Hacer del mundo un lugar mejor, y
Ser hermana de cada una de las Girl Scouts.

Living the Girl Scout Promise and Law

An important word or phrase is highlighted on each line of the Girl Scout Law. These words represent the personal characteristics of a Girl Scout. What do these words mean to you? In a troop meeting, in pairs, you could choose one line of the Girl Scout Law and take turns telling what the words mean to you. Or better yet, pick something to do that will be "living the promise." Using the words from the Girl Scout Promise and Law, create a game to share with other girls. You could also create a Girl Scout Promise and Law Good Deed Catcher. Open up your next Girl Scout meeting with the activity described at right.

Activity:

Girl Scout Good Deed Catcher

What You Do

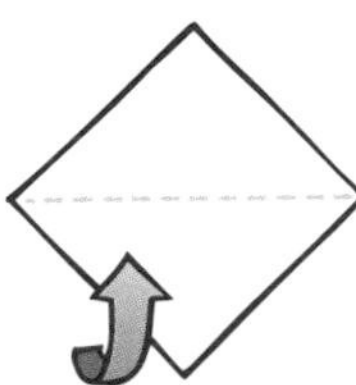

1. Start with a square piece of paper. Put it in front of you so that it looks like a diamond. Fold your paper so that the bottom corner touches the top corner. Crease and unfold.

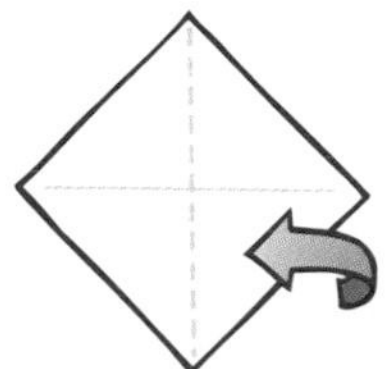

2. Fold your paper so that the right corner touches the left corner. Crease and unfold.

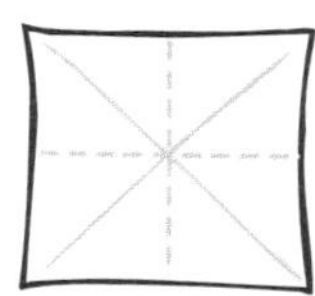

3. Fold your paper in half horizontally and vertically.

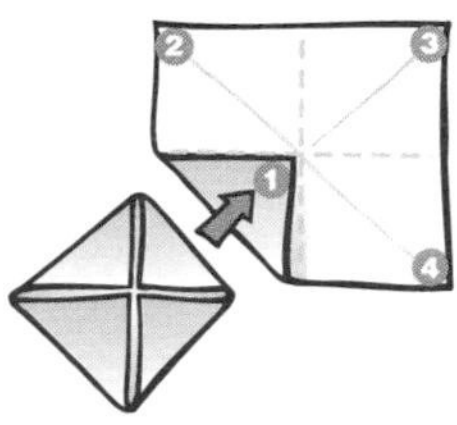

4. Starting with the bottom left corner, fold each corner in to meet the center.

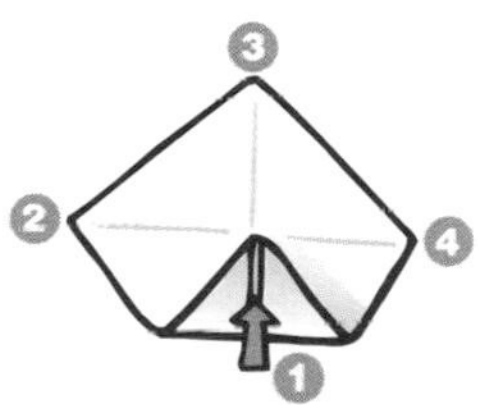

5. Turn the paper over and do the same with the other side. Fold in half.

6. Write the Girl Scout Promise on the outside four squares.

7. Write the Girl Scout Law on the inside eight triangles.

8. Under each part of the Law, write an action that represents that part of the law. Take turns with other girls "catching good deeds" that represent the meaning of the Girl Scout Promise and Law. See how many you are able to do!

Test Yourself: *Find the Meaning*

Write down what each line of the Promise means to you and discuss what you've written in your troop or group.

On my honor, I will try:	What does honor mean?
To serve God	To go along with their beliefs, some girls may choose to say a word or phrase other than God. What are some ways you can live by your beliefs?
and my country,	What are some ways you can serve your country?
To help people at all times,	What are some ways you can help people?
And to live by the Girl Scout Law.	What are some other words that mean "to live by?"

The 4 Girl Scout Program Goals

All the activities that are in your Girl Scout books are based on the four Girl Scout program goals.

one

The first program goal is for you to become the very best person you can. You should feel good about yourself and your accomplishments, be able to try new activities and be open to new challenges, and use your talents and skills in new ways.

two

The second program goal is for you to respect other people, build strong friendships, and to learn to understand and appreciate people who are different from yourself.

three

The third program goal is for you to build your own set of values that will help you to make decisions and that will guide your actions.

four

The fourth program goal is for you to build leadership skills and to contribute to your society by helping other people.

Do More

If you want to learn more about Girl Scouting, try these badges in your *Junior Girl Scout Badge Book:*

Girl Scouting Around the World

Girl Scouting in My Future

Girl Scouting in the USA

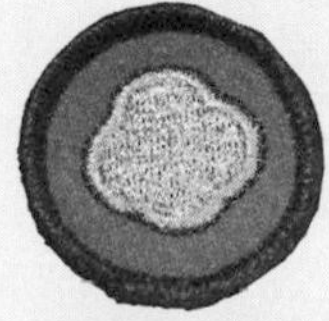

The Cookie Connection

Juliette Gordon Low understood how special words and signs help girls feel they are members of a group. Girl Scouts and Girl Guides all around the world share special signs: a handshake, the friendship squeeze, a motto, and a slogan. These special signs overcome barriers of language and culture.

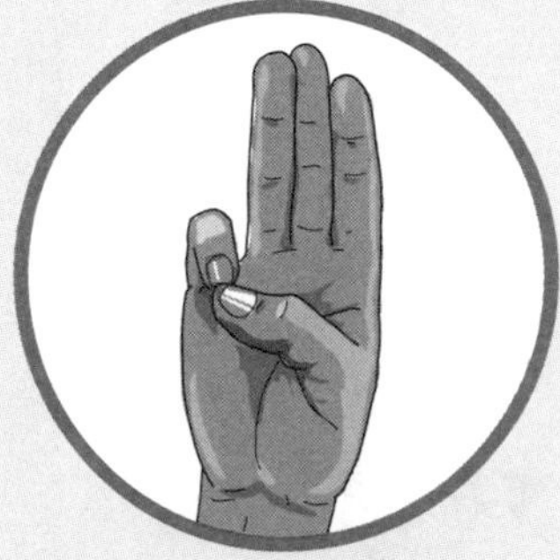

The Girl Scout Sign

This is made by raising three fingers of the right hand. This sign stands for the three parts of the Promise. You give the sign when:

- You say the Promise.
- You are welcomed into Girl Scouting at an investiture ceremony.
- You greet other Girl Scouts and Girl Guides.

The Girl Scout Handshake

This is a formal way of greeting other Girl Scouts and Girl Guides. You shake hands with the left hand and give the Girl Scout sign with your right hand.

The Quiet Sign

This is used in meetings and other gatherings to let people know it is time to stop talking. The sign is made by raising your right hand high. As people in the group see the quiet sign, they stop talking and also raise their hands. Once everyone is silent, the meeting continues.

The Friendship Circle

This stands for an unbroken chain of friendship with Girl Scouts and Girl Guides all around the world. Girl Scouts and leaders stand in a circle. Each person crosses her right arm over her left and clasps hands with her friends on both sides. Everyone makes a silent wish as a friendship squeeze is passed from hand to hand. Form a friendship circle with the girls in your group and try the friendship squeeze.

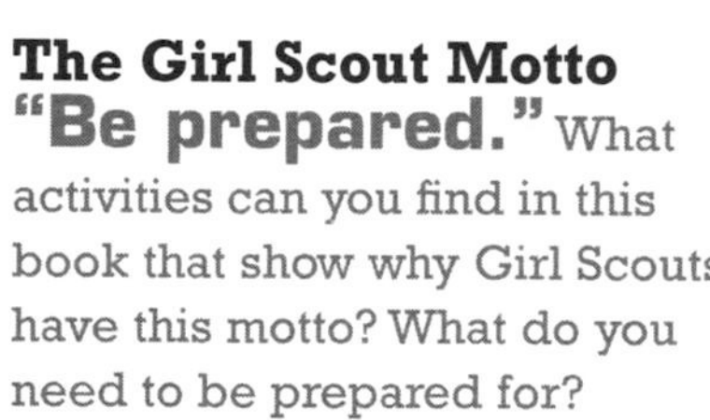

The Girl Scout Motto

"Be prepared." What activities can you find in this book that show why Girl Scouts have this motto? What do you need to be prepared for?

The Girl Scout Slogan

"Do a good turn daily." Why do you think Girl Scouts have this slogan? What kinds of good turns can you do each day?

Who can be a Girl Scout?

Any girl who is 5 through 17 years old or in kindergarten through the twelfth grade can become a Girl Scout in the United States. Girls of different races, backgrounds, and religious groups are welcome in Girl Scouting.

age levels in Girl Scouting are:

Daisy Girl Scouts
Ages 5-6 or grades K, 1

Brownie Girl Scouts
Ages 6, 7, 8 or grades 1, 2, 3

Junior Girl Scouts
Ages 8, 9, 10, 11 or grades 3, 4, 5, 6

Cadette Girl Scouts
Ages 11, 12, 13, 14 or grades 6, 7, 8, 9

Senior Girl Scouts
Ages 14, 15, 16, 17 or grades 9, 10, 11, 12

If you were a Brownie Girl Scout, as a Junior Girl Scout you will discover that girls in each level do different activities. The older you get, the more you can do. Every Girl Scout is expected to make the Girl Scout Promise and to try to live by the Girl Scout Law. And the traditions you read about on the previous page stay the same.

Adults in Girl Scouting

Adults help you carry out Girl Scout activities. You and these adults become partners. If you are participating in an activity as part of a group or troop, or if you are at a camp, event, or activity center, there will be Girl Scout leaders available. But you can also get help from family members, teachers, or clergy or community leaders.

Girl Scouts of the USA (GSUSA)

This is the national organization. The membership dues that you pay to GSUSA each year provide services to members. GSUSA creates new program activities and books, like this handbook, and operates national centers.

GSUSA also coordinates national and international events, such as wider opportunities for Cadette and Senior Girl Scouts. Read more about wider opportunities in the next chapter.

You may participate in Girl Scouting as part of a troop, camp, or interest group, or you may be an individual Girl Scout. If you are not part of a troop, you may have friends or relatives who do Girl Scout activities with you.

Girls who are registered in troops wear their troop numbers on their sashes or vests. Girls who are registered individually have their own emblem called Juliettes, which they can wear in the same spot as the troop numbers.

Juliette Gordon Low gave the girls in the earliest Girl Scout troops lots of freedom to plan the activities and projects that they wanted to do. She in turn would do her best to help them complete what they had started. That's the kind of support you should get from the adults who are helping you to enjoy your time as a Girl Scout.

The Girl Scout Council

Your Girl Scout Council is a group of women and men who make Girl Scouting happen in your area. These people have many different jobs. They may help start new troops, take care of camps, train Girl Scout leaders, or sign up new members from all parts of the community.

There are more than 300 councils in the United States today. Find out the name of your Girl Scout council. You can wear the name of your council on your uniform sash or vest.

The National Centers

Girl Scouts of the USA owns two Girl Scout national centers, each with its own special activities.

Juliette Gordon Low Girl Scout National Center, in Savannah, Georgia, is the childhood home of the founder of Girl Scouting in the United States. Many troops visit each year. You can receive more information by writing to Juliette Gordon Low Girl Scout National Center, 142 Bull Street, Savannah, Georgia 31401.

The second Girl Scout national center is the Edith Macy Conference Center, 35 miles from New York City. There, adults take classes to learn more about Girl Scouting. Camp Andree Clark, GSUSA's camp, is nearby.

Ceremonies in Girl Scouting

Special Days

Girl Scouts in the U.S.A. have four special days that are celebrated all across the nation. Girls often plan events or hold special ceremonies to celebrate these days. What events or ceremonies can you plan?

Girl Scouts at all age levels enjoy planning ceremonies. You can find many reasons to plan a ceremony. The ones that are remembered the most often have a theme, like nature, heritage, friendship, or peace. You can express the themes in many ways: through music, songs, stories, poetry, dance, or light. And some ceremonies use common symbols such as a bridge for crossing over, a dove and olive branch for peace, and green plants for nature.

Important Times for Ceremonies

- Bridging—welcomes girls into another level of Girl Scouts.
- Rededication—helps girls think about the meaning of their Girl Scout Promise and Law.
- Court of Awards—gives recognition to girls who have accomplished something (such as completing a service project, helping someone, or earning badges).
- Flag Ceremonies—are part of any program that honors the American flag.
- Fly-Up—is a bridging ceremony for Brownie Girl Scouts who are bridging to Junior Girl Scouts.
- Special Girl Scout Days—include the Girl Scout Birthday or Thinking Day.
- Investiture—is when girls welcome someone into Girl Scouting for the first time.
- Girl Scouts' Own—is an inspirational, girl-planned program to express girls' deepest feelings about something.

October 31

Juliette Gordon Low's Birthday (also known as Founder's Day)

February 22

Thinking Day, the birthday of both Lord Baden-Powell and Lady Baden-Powell. Girl Scouts and Girl Guides all over the world celebrate this day in international friendship and world peace.

March 12

The birthday of Girl Scouting in the United States of America, celebrated on or as close to the day as possible. Girl Scout Week is the week that contains March 12th. Girl Scout Sunday and Girl Scout Sabbath are in that week, too.

April 22

Girl Scout Leader's Day, when girls show their leaders how much they appreciate them.

Ceremony Worksheet

Use this as a guide for planning your own ceremonies.

Name of ceremony ______________________________

Purpose ______________________________

Theme ______________________________

Date of ceremony ____________ Time: From ____________ To ____________

Place of ceremony ______________________________

Who will attend? ______________________________

____

How will the ceremony begin? ______________________________

What songs, poems, quotations will be included? ______________________________

____

____

What activities will be included in the main part of the ceremony? ______________________________

____

____

What badges or other awards will be given? ______________________________

How will the ceremony end? ______________________________

When will a rehearsal be scheduled for the ceremony? ______________________________

Who will do each part? ______________________________

____

____

Who will record the ceremony? ______________________________

What decorations or props are needed? ______________________________

Item(s) ____________ Who will bring them? ____________

____

____

____

What refreshments will be served? ______________________________

Item(s) ____________ Who will bring them? ____________

____

____

What will the ceremony cost? ______________________________

What funds will we use? ______________________________

Who is responsible for sending thank you's? ______________________________

Girl Scout Insignia

Girl Scout insignia are all the emblems, awards, and patches that you wear on your uniform. See the picture at right for the correct placement of all your insignia.

Awards are what you earn by doing activities, such as earning a badge from the *Junior Girl Scout Badge Book.* They stand for what you have accomplished and learned in Girl Scouting.

The Girl Scout Membership Pin

Your Girl Scout Membership Pin shows others that you are a member of Girl Scouts of the USA. Its shape is called a "trefoil," and represents the three parts of the Girl Scout Promise. There are two versions of the membership pin. The newer one has three profiles inside the trefoil to show that Girl Scouting is a modern organization based on timeless values. The dark and light profiles represent the ethnic diversity (all the different races and ethnic groups) of Girl Scout membership, and the equal value placed on all girls.

The older version of the pin has the initials "GS" inside the trefoil, along with the American eagle and shield that are part of the Great Seal of the United States of America.

The World Trefoil Pin

Your blue and gold World Trefoil Pin shows that you are part of a worldwide movement of Girl Guides and Girl Scouts. The blue stands for the sky and the gold stands for the sun. The trefoil stands for the three parts of the Girl Scout Promise. The base of the trefoil is shaped like a flame, which represents the love of humanity and the flame that burns in the hearts of Girl Guides and Girl Scouts around the world. The line in the middle of the trefoil stands for the compass needle that guides us, while the two stars stand for the Promise and Law.

Religious Awards

Many religious groups have special awards for Girl Scouts of their faith. If you wish to earn one of these awards, your Girl Scout council, Girl Scout leader, or religious group can tell you more about it. These can be worn below the membership stars.

Troop Number and Troop Crest

Your troop or group number and troop or group crest show the Girl Scout troop or group of which you are a member. The council strip shows the Girl Scout council where you are a member.

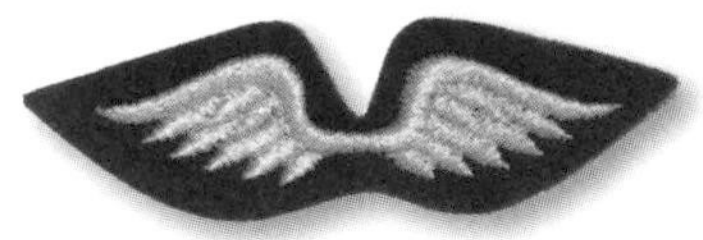

Brownie Girl Scout Wings

Brownie Girl Scouts who become Junior Girl Scouts "fly up." Brownie Girl Scout Wings are worn to show that you have flown up.

Membership Stars and Discs

You get a membership star and disc for each year that you are a member of Girl Scouting.

- The blue disc is for Daisy Girl Scouts.
- The green disc is for Brownie Girl Scouts.
- The yellow disc is for Junior Girl Scouts.
- The white disc is for Cadette and Senior Girl Scouts.

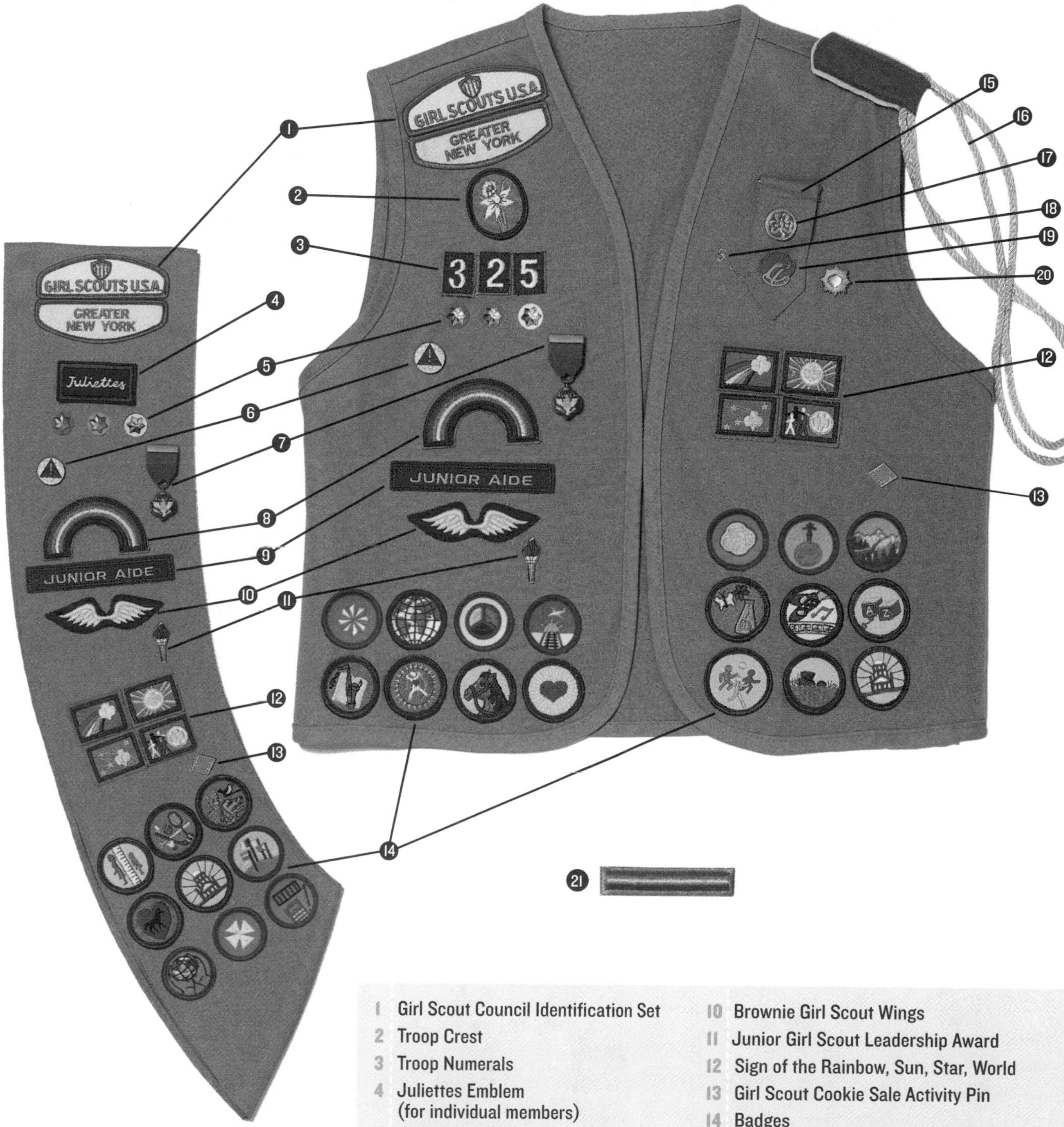

GIRL SCOUTS U.S.A.
GREATER NEW YORK
Juliettes
325
JUNIOR AIDE

1	Girl Scout Council Identification Set
2	Troop Crest
3	Troop Numerals
4	Juliettes Emblem (for individual members)
5	Membership Disc and Star (Daisy–blue, Brownies–green, Junior–yellow)
6	Safety Award
7	Medal of Honor Lifesaving Award
8	Bridge to Junior Girl Scouts
9	Junior Aide Award
10	Brownie Girl Scout Wings
11	Junior Girl Scout Leadership Award
12	Sign of the Rainbow, Sun, Star, World
13	Girl Scout Cookie Sale Activity Pin
14	Badges
15	Junior Girl Scout Insignia Tab
16	Patrol Leader's Cord
17	World Trefoil Pin
18	Membership Numeral Guard
19	Girl Scout Membership Pin
20	Girl Scout Bronze Award
21	Bridge to Cadette Girl Scouts

The Junior Girl Scout Uniform

Just like wearing your Girl Scout Membership Pin, wearing a uniform is another way of showing that you belong to an organization. Your uniform was designed with the comments and suggestions of Junior Girl Scouts around the country.

You are not required to own a uniform, but many girls who have one like to wear it to participate in ceremonies, attend an event as part of a Girl Scout group, attend an event on a special Girl Scout day, or attend regular meetings.

The Junior Girl Scout uniform has different pieces that you can mix or match. These pictures show the different styles of the Junior Girl Scout uniform.

Activity:

Insignia Relay Race

In your troop, divide into two teams. Each team should have the exact same set of insignia. Have a relay race to see which team can place its set of insignia on a sash or vest correctly in the shortest amount of time. You can try this by yourself using a timer to see how quickly you can place the awards in the right spots.

Girl Scouts Are Global

Girl Scouts of the USA is one of many Girl Scout/Girl Guide organizations around the world. Together, these organizations have nine million Girl Scouts and Girl Guides in about 140 countries that stretch around the globe. They are joined together in an international organization called the World Association of Girl Guides and Girl Scouts (WAGGGS).

Each of the WAGGGS countries have Girl Scout or Girl Guide troops similar to your troop. The girls in these troops around the world are your Girl Scout/Girl Guide sisters.

This means that as a member of Girl Scouts of the USA, you are also a member of WAGGGS. Your World Trefoil Pin shows that you are a part of this global organization.

The Girl Scout Promise

▶ IN INDONESIA

Tri Satya

Demi kehormatanku aku berjanji akan
Bersungguh-sungguh
• menjalankan kewajibanku terhadap
Tuhan dan Negara Kesatuna Republik
Indonesia, dan menjalankan Pancasila;
• menolong sesama hidup dan
mempersiapkan diri membangun masyarakat;
• menepati Dasa Darma.

The English version

Promise

On my honor I promise that I will do my best:
To do my duty to God, and to the Republic of Indonesia and to carry out Pancasila,
To help all living beings and be ready to
Build up the nation,
To obey the Dasa Darma.

The Girl Scout Law

▶ IN THE NETHERLANDS

Wet

Een padvindster/gids trekt er samen met
Anderen op uit om de wereld om zich
Heen te ontdekken en deze meer leefaar
te maken.
Zij is eerlijk, trovw en houdt vol.
Zij is spaarzaam en sober en heeft zorg
voor de natuur.
Zij ressecteert zichzelf en anderen.

The English version

Law

A Girl Guide goes out with others in order
To discover the world around her and make it more worthwhile to live in.
She is honest, faithful, and perseveres.
She is thrifty and sober and takes good care of nature.
She respects herself and others.

The World Centers

WAGGGS has four world centers. The Cabaña is in Cuernavaca, Mexico; the Chalet is in Adelboden, Switzerland; Pax Lodge is at the Olave Center in London, England; and Sangam is in Pune, India.

Through international wider opportunities, Cadette and Senior Girl Scouts can visit these centers and take part in many activities. As a registered Girl Scout, you and your family can also stay at these centers on a visit to these countries if you have made arrangements ahead of time. For more information, visit the Girl Scout Web site or write to the Membership Program, and Diversity Group, World Centers Information, Girl Scouts of the USA, 420 Fifth Avenue, New York, New York 10018-2798.

International Friendship

The founder of Girl Scouts of the USA, Juliette Gordon Low, believed in international friendship and cooperation. After her death in 1927, a special fund was created to be "dedicated forever to good will and cooperation among the nations of the world." How would you like to continue the work of Juliette Gordon Low? You can, and you do, every time you give to the Juliette Low World Friendship Fund.

Here is what can happen when Girl Scouts give to the Juliette Low World Friendship Fund:

- Mercedes learns first aid skills at a class, and later teaches her troop in El Salvador. She decides she wants to become a doctor.
- Yanti, from Malaysia, and Tatiana, from Russia, meet at a camping event and build a lifetime friendship.

Become a Global Thinker

These girls are global thinkers. They cooperate with each other to improve their lives and help people around the globe. You can be a global thinker, too. Find out about a problem that affects girls in another country. Discuss with your troop and your leader how you can help other girls grow strong.

For general information on international Girl Scouting, start with the World Association of Girl Guides and Girl Scouts' Web site *www.wagggs.org*. Also visit the Girl Scouts' "Just for Girls" page *www.girlscouts.org*.

Earn a Global Patch

You can receive the "Girl Scouts Go Global" patch by doing some activities in a booklet by the same name. Look for more information on the Girl Scout Web site, or contact your Girl Scout council.

Do More

If you are interested in reaching out internationally, try these badges in your *Junior Girl Scout Badge Book:*

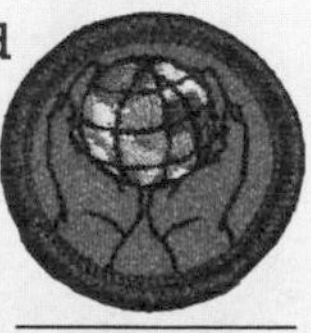

Global Awareness

Humans and Habitats

Traveler

World Neighbors

Celebrating People

Globe Trotting

2 Adventures in Girl Scouting

In This Chapter You Will Learn About:

One of the best parts of being a Junior Girl Scout is looking ahead to the adventures you will have now, next month, and next year. In Girl Scouting you can do activities that might be totally new to you—such as camping, wider opportunities, and service projects—and you can build on hobbies and interests that you already have. In Girl Scouting you learn and do today what you can do even more of—with greater skill and challenges—tomorrow.

Group Leadership

Girls in Girl Scouting make it happen. They plan, decide, work together, and have fun. You will get to practice being a leader in many ways. You will also learn how to work in a group.

A good working group has to have people in it who are good at many different things. Here are some of the things leaders and group members do.

Direct.
Introduce ideas, encourage everyone to accept responsibility.

Listen.
Collect information and summarize important ideas so the group can make the best decision.

Support.
Help everyone to be a part of the group and help the group reach its goals.

Spread the word.
Express the thoughts and decisions of the group. Spread the important news.

Make peace.
Don't let arguments get out of hand. Find compromises everyone can accept.

Write it down.
Keep track of the important stuff.

Manage money
Plan and keep track of the budget and treasury.

Getting Groups on Track

Sometimes when a group tries to make decisions or plan an activity, the group members might not agree. Conflict resolution is a good technique to use when people disagree. Follow these steps:

1. **Figure out what the problem is.**
   Example: Every member of the group wants to do a different activity in the handbook.

2. **Suggest some solutions to the problem.**
   Example: Each girl could take a turn choosing an activity for the whole group. Or the names of activities could go in a container, and the one selected is the first one this group will do. Or the girls might work in smaller groups on different activities, choosing one activity for each group. Or each girl could do her own thing and work on activities independently.

3. **Look at what would happen with each solution.**
   Example: Talk about each way to go. You could list the good points and bad points of each.

4. **Make a decision.**
   Example: The girls in the group decide to split into smaller groups. Each small group picks an activity that interests its members. It is decided that later the entire group will work together on a service project and on planning a trip.

5. **Take action.**
   Example: The plan is put into action. Some girls start with activities in Chapter Four; others go directly to Chapter Seven.

Do you have a conflict going on in your troop or group? Try using the above steps and see if they help you resolve it.

WHAT'S *Not* GOOD FOR THE GROUP

YELL!

Tell lies

Criticize

DISCRIMINATE

Embarrass

Be untrustworthy

PLAY FAVORITES

GOSSIP

Be undependable

A Troop Code of Conduct
Draw up a troop code of conduct that everyone signs.

We will:

We won't:

Signatures:

Test Yourself: *What does this group need?*

In each of these examples, decide what is needed to help the group.

- Your troop is hoping to go on a trip. Everyone has a different idea about where to go and how to pay for it.
- Two girls disagree on which activities the troop should do during their camping trip.
- The troop is planning a trip to the Juliette Gordon Low National Center, but it is going to take some money.
- A service project is planned to collect clothing and toiletries to donate to a local homeless shelter.
- It's the first meeting of the troop year. Some girls have really strong ideas about what to do. Others are totally quiet.

What Makes a Leader?

Leadership means to show the way; to guide or cause others to follow you; to direct; to be in charge. Every group has a leader. And it doesn't always have to be the same person all the time.

Junior Girl Scouts can be leaders in many ways. Maybe you are a leader on a sports team, in your social studies class, or in the youth group at your place of worship. Maybe you are a teacher's assistant or you have younger siblings or cousins who look up to you.

Perhaps you helped plan a family reunion or taught someone how to solve a math problem. If you think about it, you can probably come up with more than one situation where you were a leader. List all of the ways you are a leader, and all of the skills you use in each leadership situation.

Try to take on a new leadership role for a month or so in your troop, school, or community. This might mean becoming a leader on a sports team, an art project, or a music group.

Troop Leadership

Leaders have . . .

- Creativity
- Ideas
- Determination
- Commitment
- Humor
- Enthusiasm
- Respect for others
- Fair-mindedness
- Organizational skills
- Decision-making skills
- Inspiration
- Teaching ability
- Goals
- Solutions
- Negotiating skills
- Support
- Power
- Time-management skills

Your Junior Girl Scout troop is the perfect place to practice and strengthen your leadership skills. When Juliette Gordon Low was a leader, it was not common for women to assume leadership beyond the family. Nor was it common for a person with a disability to lead others. Juliette Gordon Low was a memorable leader. She loved what she was doing, and one reason that girls and adults followed her was because she had a sense of humor and a great feel for adventure. She also was known for her ability to begin something, then step back and let others take over after she was sure they were on the right track.

Being a Leader in Troop Government

Along with your Girl Scout leader, you and the other girls in your troop can set up a system for troop government. This will give you many opportunities to play a leadership role.

See on the opposite page the three models of troop or group government used most often by Junior Girl Scouts. Which system would work best for achieving your troop's goals? What role would you like to have in your troop government?

If you are not in a troop that meets with the same set of girls on a regular basis, you can still find many ways to be a leader in Girl Scouts. You can offer to assist a Daisy or Brownie Girl Scout troop, or plan a service project or a leadership action project. (See details later in this chapter.)

Three Models of Troop Government

	Patrol	Executive Board	Town Meeting
HOW IT IS ORGANIZED	The troop divides into small groups called patrols. (Good for medium to large troops)	One leadership team is elected to represent the entire troop. (Good for smaller troops)	The troop has no formal government. The entire troop participates directly in the decision-making process.
HOW IT WORKS	Patrols choose patrol name, patrol symbol, patrol leaders, and assistant patrol leaders. A kaper chart lists jobs and who does them.	The troop elects girls to the leadership team, which sometimes is called the steering committee. The team then elects its officers (President, Secretary, Treasurer). The number of officers varies with the projects.	Troop business is discussed and determined by all girls in the troop. This system requires a moderator. The moderator guides troop discussion.
HOW LONG IT LASTS	Members of the patrol should rotate the leadership jobs so that everyone has an opportunity.	The length of time in leadership positions should be limited to give each girl an opportunity to lead.	Rotate the moderator position so everyone gets a chance to lead.

Court of Honor

The Girl Scout leader, the patrol leaders, and the troop secretary and treasurer make up the Court of Honor. Not every troop has a Court of Honor—usually only larger troops use it. The secretary takes notes at troop or group meetings and keeps these notes as a record of what was discussed. The treasurer tracks troop or group dues and other Girl Scout money and supplies. In some large troops, each patrol might have its own secretary and treasurer.

Court of Honor meetings are held before or after regular troop meetings. The Court of Honor comes up with plans and ideas for the patrols to discuss and vote on. The Court of Honor also asks for ideas and suggestions from patrols, and sets up and maintains a troop kaper chart that outlines assignments for each patrol.

Choosing Leaders

Whenever you choose girls as leaders for troop government positions, think about how you are making your choices. Think about being fair. Think about what it takes to be a leader.

Managing Money

In addition to developing leadership abilities, Girl Scouting gives you the opportunity to learn another important skill: managing money.

By learning how to manage your money, you can figure out how to earn, save, and spend money wisely. Here are four ways you can develop your money management skills as a Girl Scout.

1. **Money-Earning Projects**
   In Junior Girl Scouts, you make lots of decisions about how to earn and use money. Whether you are in a troop or group, or are registered individually, most Girl Scouts participate in money-earning projects and make decisions about using these funds. You might need money for all kinds of things: project supplies, trips, games, books, equipment, and donations, for example. Money from dues or earned through special projects can be spent on Girl Scout activities, but because there is not an unlimited supply, you have to plan a budget carefully.

2. **Managing the Troop or Group Dues**
   Dues are the money each group member agrees to contribute to your troop or group. Dues should be an amount that everyone can afford. There is no one best amount.

   As a Girl Scout, you will make many decisions about your dues: How often will dues be collected? Who will collect them? Where will the money be kept? How will the dues be spent? It's up to you and your troop to decide. If you are saving for a special project, your troop might decide to raise the dues for awhile. If you have enough money saved up, the troop might lower the dues.

3. **Keeping Track of the Money**
   Your troop or group needs an easy and clear way to keep track of its money. The money you collect is called *income.* The things you spend your money on are called *expenses.* Every time money is collected, you will add to your total. When your troop decides to spend money, it will be recorded too. A new total must be figured out.

   On the opposite page is a sample of how to record the money that comes in and goes out of your troop.

4. **Becoming the Troop Treasurer**
   You might want to be your troop's treasurer, who is in charge of keeping track of the income and expenses. The treasurer should give a report about how much money the troop has. Keep your troop's money in a safe place. The best place is a bank.

Do More

If this section about Money Management interests you, check out this badge in your *Junior Girl Scout Badge Book.*

Money Sense

A Troop Budget

INCOME

Income	
Dues	
Product Sales	
Money-Earning Projects	
Contributions (from parents, sponsors, etc.)	
Money from Last Year	
Other	
Total Income	

EXPENSES

Expenses	
Supplies	
Transportation	
Fees (for example, for admissions)	
Refreshments (food and drinks)	
Awards	
Other	
Total Expenses	

TOTAL

Total	
Total Income	
– Total Expenses	
New Total	

Making Money

Selling Girl Scout Cookies

The Girl Scout cookie sale is a way many Girl Scouts earn money for troop activities, from trips to service projects. If you decide to work on the Girl Scout cookie sale, there are many different ways to be involved. You can sell cookies. You can help organize cookie boxes. You can keep track of the money.

There are decisions to make about the best way to sell the most cookies. Maybe you could sell cookies at a shopping mall or in the lobby of an office building. It's up to you, the members of your troop or group, your leader, and your parents to decide.

The Rules of Selling

The following things need to happen before you start selling cookies:

- You need to get permission from your parents or guardians.
- Your troop or group should discuss safety rules.
- Your troop or group should discuss what you plan to do with the money you earn.
- You need to practice your sales skills. Think of different situations and what you might say to a customer.

Smart Ways to Sell

What makes a good sales person? Here are some tips.

- Know your cookies! Be able to answer customers' questions.
- Know what your Girl Scout troop or group is planning to do with the money it earns.
- Give customers the facts! Let the customer know how much money she owes you, when you will be collecting this money, and when you will deliver the cookies and other products.
- Be polite. Always say thank you, even if someone doesn't buy anything. People will remember your good manners, which is important because you are representing Girl Scouts as well as yourself.
- Follow through. Deliver the cookies and other products on the day promised.

Other Money-Earning Projects

Look at the list of ideas below for the many ways that Girl Scout troops and groups can earn money. Which ideas capture your interest? Can you think of other ideas?

- Baby-sitting
- Gift-wrapping
- Car or bike washing
- Weeding, raking leaves, lawn mowing, or other lawn work
- Organizing a recycling drive
- Selling crafts or baked goods. See the "Create and Invent" chapter for things you can make to sell
- Pet-sitting, plant-sitting, or dog walking
- Coupon clipping: convince your family to give you the difference between the full price and coupon price for each coupon used!
- Selling used toys: sell off your unwanted toys for cash!

Follow the "Rules of Selling" on this page before beginning these projects.

Activity:

Repairing a Bike Chain

Bike chains slip off—usually when you're trying to get somewhere fast. They aren't hard to fix. You can even set up a bike clinic and raise some cash by fixing chains, or by teaching other kids how to fix their own. Have an adult show you how to fix a flat as well.

Step 

If your bike has a derailleur (the device for shifting gears that uses chains), thread the chain through it.

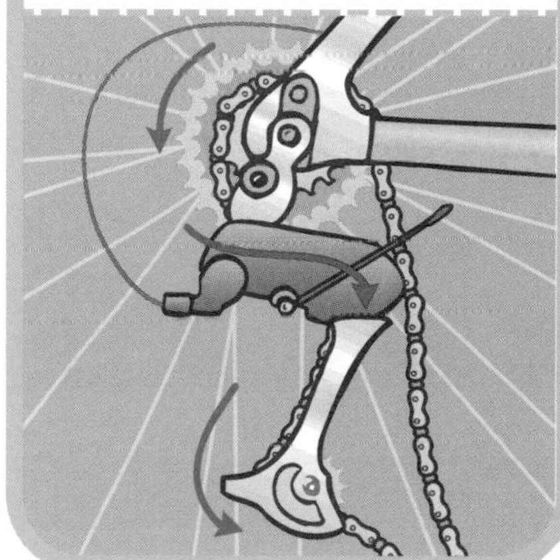

Step 

Thread the bike chain through the hub in the back.

Step 

Turn the pedals—go slowly—and ease the chain onto the sprockets.

Step 

Carry the chain to the top of the front pedal's sprocket.

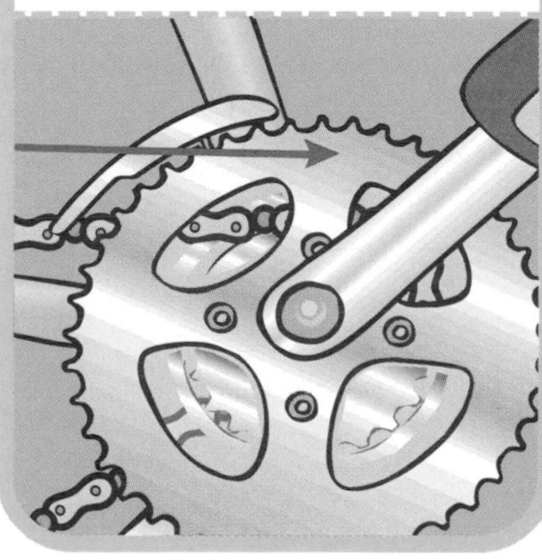

Create a Budget

You might find it hard to make your money last, but it's a lot easier if you have a budget. A budget helps you make sure you have the money you need (income) for the things you want (expenses). For example, if you set a goal to buy a new sweater that costs $30, but you've only got $20, you know you've got to save another $10 before you can buy it. If you spend $5 of your savings on candy and video games one day after school, now you've got to save $15!

Coming up with a budget can help you see how much money you need to set aside each day or week—and how much you can spend—in order to reach your goal.

How to Have Money for What You Want

It's not hard to come up with a budget. Check out the budget sheet below. *Fixed* expenses are those things you spend your money on that you *cannot* control, such as school lunch or troop dues. *Flexible* expenses are those things you spend your money on that you *can* control, such as snacks, clothes, or magazines.

To use the budget sheet, fill in the amount of money you expect to get each week—from your allowance, any jobs you might have, or gifts. Then record the amount you plan to spend on fixed and flexible expenses. At the end of the week, write in the amount you actually spent. How well did you stick to your budget?

If you are not saving as much money as you would like to, you have two choices:

1. Cut back on your flexible expenses.
2. Try to earn more money! (See the previous two pages for money-earning projects.)

		Week 1		Week 2		Week 3	
	INCOME: Money I expect from allowance, jobs, gifts.						
	Total Income						
	EXPENSES: Money I expect to spend.						
		Planned	Spent	Planned	Spent	Planned	Spent
Fixed Expenses	School lunch						
	Transportation						
	Troop dues						
	________						
Flexible Expenses	Snacks						
	Movies						
	Music						
	Video games						
	Magazines						
	Other						
	Savings						
	Donations						
	________						

WIDER OPS

A wider opportunity is an activity that takes you and your Girl Scout friends to a new place. It can be simple—like visiting a farm, exploring a museum, hiking someplace new—or it can be a special weekend event where you sleep away from home.

Wider opportunities can also be national events that appear each year in the booklet *Wider Ops.* Ask your Girl Scout leader to bring a copy of *Wider Ops* to a troop or group meeting. Look through it and find three wider opportunities you think you would enjoy when you are a Cadette or Senior Girl Scout. These events are open only to Cadette and Senior Girl Scouts. But Junior Girl Scouts can look forward to these as they continue in Girl Scouting. The activities you do now can prepare you to attend one of the national events when you are a Cadette or Senior Girl Scout. Doing the activities in this book and in the *Junior Girl Scout Badge Book* will give you lots of chances to plan your own wider opportunities.

Learning More About Wider Ops

Invite a teen Girl Scout or someone from your Girl Scout council to talk to you and your friends about a wider opportunity. Find out which events and workshops you can attend as a Junior Girl Scout.

Learn about wider opportunities now offered by Girl Scout councils. Remember, you don't have to wait until you're a Cadette Girl Scout to have a travel experience. There are opportunities for travel and adventure in your town and surrounding areas.

Go Girl! A Travel Action Plan

Fun! Adventure! Safety! Learn how to plan well to get the most from your Girl Scout trip or service project. Where do you start? What do you need to know? Follow the *Go Girl!* plan outlined here. It takes more than one meeting to do all of the steps, but in the end, you'll have a skill you can use over and over again.

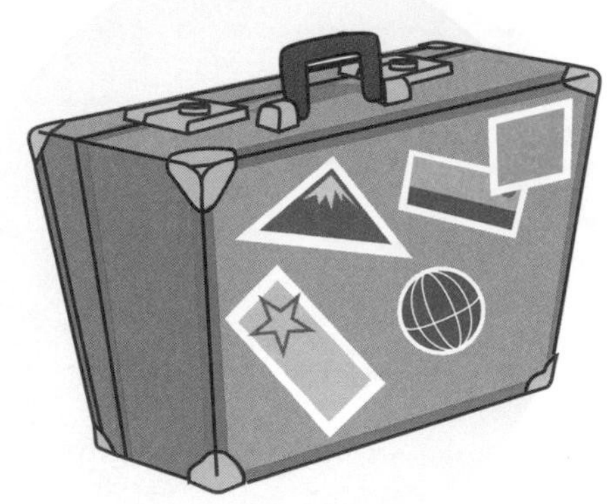

Step 1:
Where in the World?

Listed below are some idea-starters for places you and your friends might like to visit or enjoy.

- Library
- Park
- Zoo or wildlife center
- Government office
- Veterinarian office
- Science or nature center
- Farm or orchard

Brainstorm a list of things you'd like to do or see. Decide which of the suggestions on your list you'd like to do and express them as a concrete action. For example:

- Read to your younger siblings or to younger Girl Scouts at your local library.
- Take a nature hike.
- Go to the zoo.
- Have a sports day at the park.
- Do a community service project.
- Go to a Girl Scout camp.
- Plan a visit to a nearby historical site.
- Develop your Girl Scout plans for the year.

	Choice 1:	Choice 2:	Choice 3:
cost			
money-earning activities			
transportation			
uniforms			
activity			
meals			
reservations			
expected weather			
approvals needed			

Step 2:
So Many Choices!

When you and the other girls in your troop have narrowed your list to two to five possible activities, you are now ready to plan. With the group's top choices, discuss:

1. How much will it cost?
2. How can you raise money or get financial help?
3. How will you get there?
4. What will you do when you get there?
5. What do you need to bring?
6. Will you travel in uniform?
7. How will you get your meals?
8. When is the best time to go? The best time to return home?
9. Do you need to make reservations or get permission to visit the place?
10. Will the weather affect your plans?
11. Do you need approval from your Girl Scout council?
12. What guidelines should you follow in your leader's copy of *Safety-Wise*?
13. How many adults need to go along?

Once you have answers you can decide what you want to do and when.

The best choice for your trip is

________________________________.

Step 3:
What's Up?

Learn about the place you plan to visit. Write or telephone the Visitors' Center or Chamber of Commerce of the town. Many have a Web site to visit. Ask for maps, a calendar of events, and tourist brochures. If you're staying local, making a phone call might be all you need to do.

Step 4:
Money Can Be Funny!

1. Calculate how much the trip will cost. Make a list of everything you expect to pay for and estimate how much each thing will cost. Include meals, transportation, equipment, materials, and admission and/or ticket fees. Use a chart or graph to list all the costs for your outing.
2. Decide how you will pay for the trip. Is this trip covered by money in the troop treasury? Will you need to plan a special money-earning project so that everyone can go?

Step 5:
Permission Please!

You must get written permission from your parent or guardian before going on any trip. You must also have enough adults to go with you. Your Girl Scout leader will help work out the details.

Step 6:
The Perfect Fit

Determine ahead of time special clothing and equipment to bring and make a list. Learn about rolling or packing clothes carefully to fit into a suitcase, sleeping bag, or knapsack.

Step 7:
Sign the Safe Passenger Pledge

You will find the pledge in the book *Safety-Wise*, which is your leader's safety manual for Girl Scout activities. Work with your leader to follow the directions in *Safety-Wise*.

Step 8:
On the Road

Review a map of the place you plan to visit to figure out exactly how to get there. Decide what you want to see along the way and after you arrive. Is there anything particular to visit or see, such as scenic landscapes, historic towns, or other points of interest? Remember to bring the map with you on your trip!

Promoting Peace

As you travel more and become acquainted with different people, you will have an opportunity to promote peace in the world. It's up to you: What does it mean to be a peacemaker? What are the risks involved? What are the rewards? Design a way to express what the world would be like at peace. Or, make your own peace pole, with the word "Peace," or the phrase "May Peace Prevail on Earth" written on four sides of a pole.

Peace Poles are four-sided wooden pillars inscribed with the words "May Peace Prevail on Earth" in at least four different languages. They have been placed all over the world to remind people to think about peace.

Place the pole in a quiet place where people can reflect on what peace means. Suggestions: in a public garden or at camp.

Here are some ways of saying peace in different languages:

Amami	Swahili
Frieden	German
Heiwa	Japanese
Heping	Mandarin
Mir	Russian
Paix	French
Salaam	Arabic
Shalom	Hebrew
Shanti	Sanskrit
Wokiyapi	Sioux
Paz	Spanish

Do More

If you are interested in learning more about different cultures, try these badges in your *Junior Girl Scout Badge Book:*

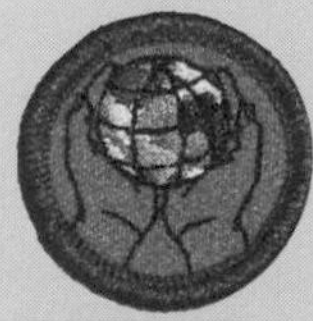

Global Awareness

Humans and Habitats

On My Way

Traveler

World Neighbors

May Peace Prevail on Earth
Que reine la paz en la Tierra

A Girl Scout travel tradition is to give and receive swaps whenever a group of Girl Scouts from different places get together. Swaps show something special about you and where you are from. You can get many ideas for swaps from the activities in this book. See the "Create and Invent" chapter for ideas or try the ones on these two pages.

Activity:

My Native Rock Necklace

What You Need
- Twine
- A rock for each necklace
- Glue

What You Do
1. Collect rocks from a special place in your community.
2. Cut one yard of twine for each necklace.
3. Bend twine in half and place a dab of glue at the fold and attach to the back of the rock.
4. Wrap twine around rock, gluing where needed.
5. Tie ends together to make the necklace.

You could paint the rock with something that represents where you are from, like the name of your Girl Scout council, or a scene or symbol of your troop or state, before wrapping it with twine.

Activity:

Petal Pins and Pendants

What You Need

- Clear plastic with an adhesive back, or wide, clear plastic tape
- Large safety pins or earring findings or chains (available at arts and crafts stores)
- Small- to medium-sized flowers and leaves (not wildflowers, and only gathered with permission)
- Paper towels and a heavy book (for pressing the flowers)
- Scissors
- Floral wire

What You Do

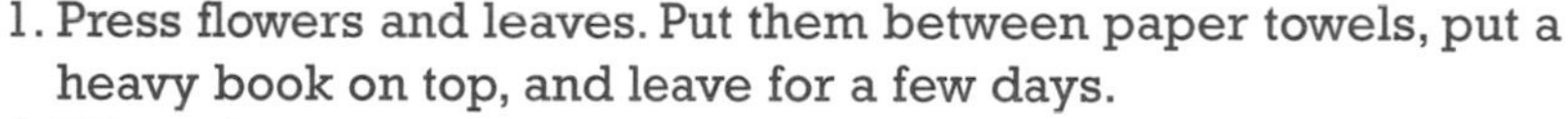

1. Press flowers and leaves. Put them between paper towels, put a heavy book on top, and leave for a few days.

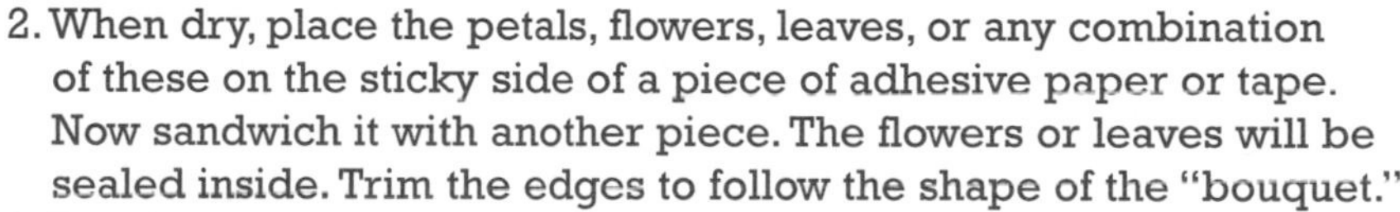

2. When dry, place the petals, flowers, leaves, or any combination of these on the sticky side of a piece of adhesive paper or tape. Now sandwich it with another piece. The flowers or leaves will be sealed inside. Trim the edges to follow the shape of the "bouquet."

3. Punch a small hole in the top and put a loop of floral wire through the hole.
4. String a chain, safety pin, or earring finding through the floral wire.
5. If it is being used as a swap, make labels. Write on pieces of paper or type on a computer (use a small font) the name of your council as many times as you will have pieces of jewelry. Cut the labels apart. Lay each label behind the flower/leaf arrangement before sealing so it can be read from the back.

Being an Active Citizen

One of the most important things that Girl Scouts do is to help others. Girl Scouts all over the United States and around the world do service projects. Doing a service project helps you develop your leadership skills. Active citizens care for and improve the place they live.

Sometimes it's easier not to act. For example, if the corner trash can is full, it is easier to throw a candy wrapper on the ground than walk another block to find an empty trash can or write the sanitation department and ask them to empty the trash cans more often. But think about what kind of mess there would be if lots of people threw their trash on the ground! That is why citizens need to act to identify and solve community problems.

Your Own Action Plan

Here are the steps you need to follow to create your own service project. Use the following action plan outline.

1. Brainstorm ideas

What can you do to help others? Create a list of ideas in a brainstorming session.

2. Decide

Write down the final idea you chose.

3. Get information

Always ask who, what, when, where, why, and how.

- Why are you doing this project?
- What are you going to do?
- What equipment do you need?
- Who will help?
- Who do you need to ask permission of?
- Who do you need to work with?
- When can you start?
- Where will you meet?
- How much will it cost, if anything?
- How will you pay for it?
- How will you get there?
- How will you know if you did a good job?

4. Plan

Make a list of everyone you need to meet with. Write down their names and the date of your meeting. Give yourself a start and finish date for the project.

5. Put your ideas into action

Write down the name of every person or committee who is working on the project, and what they are responsible for.

6. Evaluate what was done

- What did you like about the project?
- What would you do differently?
- Think about if you would or would not do the project again and why.

7. Share your success

- Make a list of everyone you need to send a thank-you note to, then do it.
- Make a plan for how to celebrate your success.
- Tell your Girl Scout Council about your success. Are there other groups or people you should tell?

How to Be a Leader

- What leadership skills did you use to plan a trip?
- To go on the trip?
- To plan a service project?
- To carry out a service project?

You can be a leader in many ways: the person who thinks up the idea, the person who keeps the project on track, the person who helps others get along. Your troop or group members and your Girl Scout leader are there to help you discover your unique way of leading. The choice is yours and so is the fun!

Do More

If this section interests you, try these badges in your *Junior Girl Scout Badge Book:*

Lead On

Model Citizen

My Community

3 It's Great to Be a Girl

In This Chapter You Will Learn About:

You are probably noticing that a lot of things in your life are changing. Some changes are great and exciting, like getting a bigger allowance and more freedom, for example. Some changes might be a little confusing, such as having to make tough decisions and having more responsibility. Your body is changing too, and your feelings might seem to be on a roller-coaster ride.

Luckily for you, Junior Girl Scouts is a terrific group to belong to while all this change is happening. Your Junior Girl Scout sisters are ready to listen and share their own growing-up tales. It's nice to know you are not alone.

You also have your Junior Girl Scout leaders and other adults who have gone through this growing-up thing themselves. They are here to help you with good advice and time to listen—take advantage of them!

You have all the activities that you do as a Junior Girl Scout—in this handbook, in other Girl Scout books, and on the "Just for Girls" Web site. Why are these helpful? As you grow up, your likes, interests, values, and relationships can change again and again. As a Junior Girl Scout, you can try different types of activities and learn a lot about yourself and what you like to do. You can try a challenge or something new and know you are with people who support you.

What's in a Name?

Lots of Junior Girl Scouts get "camp names"—nicknames—the first time they go to camp. Some keep these nicknames every year they attend camp. Do you have a nickname? Would you like one? Would you like a new one?

You and the girls in your troop or group can make up special nicknames to use when you do Girl Scout activities. The best nicknames say something about who you are and what you like to do. Brainstorm with your friends to come up with names for each of you.

[Bonus: What American founder of the world's largest organization for girls was nicknamed "Daisy"?]

WHO AM I

What kind of person are you? On this page you will think about that question and answer it. You can use this information to introduce yourself to the girls in your group or troop. Write down your answers on a separate piece of paper, because your answers will probably change during your time in Girl Scouts. Don't worry about filling in all the blanks—this is not a test! You can't be right or wrong—just yourself!

My name is ______________________________.

My nickname is ____________ because ____________.

I am ____________ years old and in ____________ grade.

My favorite sport to play is ____________________.

I like it because ______________________________.

My favorite subject in school is ________________.

I like it because ______________________________.

My favorite hobby is ___________________________.

My favorite thing to do with my family is ____________

____

My favorite thing to do with my friends is ____________.

____

My favorite music is ___________________________.

One thing I do really well is ____________________.

Two things that I don't do as well as I would like are:

______________________ and ____________________.

The best part of my day is when I ________________.

What bugs me the most: _________________________

Three words that describe the best things about me are:

____

Three words that describe the worst things about me are:

1. ______________________________

2. ______________________________

3. ______________________________

The best word to describe my family is ____________.

There are __________ people in my family. ______ live with me and ____________ do not live with me.

I have ________ pets. Their names are ____________.

OR

I don't have a pet, but I'd like to have a ________ as a pet.

I'd call it ______________________.

The best word to describe me and my best friend is ____.

We love to talk about ______________________.

One time we had a fight about ______________________.

We made up when ______________________

______________________________________.

One more thing I would like to share about myself is

____

______________________________________.

NOW?

What Do You Value?

Test yourself by answering these three questions:

1. You are going to try to survive on a deserted island that has plenty of food and water. You can only bring five things. What would you bring and why?
2. What do you like the most about your best friend? Why?
3. Zap! Your fairy godmother has made you a one-time offer: Do you want great athletic skill or incredible singing talent? Which do you pick? You have ten seconds, starting now—ten, nine, eight, seven, six, five, four, three, two, one . . . .

Did you have to think about your answers a bit? That's because your answers show some of your values. Values are those things that are important to you, the things in which you strongly believe.

Listening to Your Heart

Your values affect how you behave or see things. For example, if you and your family place a high value on education, you might not care that you don't get a big allowance—you know your family is saving money for your college education.

Values help you make decisions. They help you use information and decide what you should do based on your own personal beliefs. Your values start to take shape with the help of your family. Your spiritual beliefs, your friends, television and movies, the music you listen to, your community, and your education all have an impact on your values.

Your values influence your behavior. For example, if being a great dancer or athlete is important to you, you probably value fitness. You wouldn't do harmful things to your body (smoke, do drugs), because that would get in the way of you becoming the best athlete you can be. If you sometimes act in a way that is not in line with your values—maybe you try a cigarette one day—you will probably feel uncomfortable. Staying true to who you are—knowing what your values are—can help you make good decisions.

Test Yourself: *What's right? What's wrong?*

You have $10 that you'd like to donate to a local charity. You can't make up your mind about which group to give it to. You would like to make a contribution to a group that provides food to the homeless, but you would also like to give the money to the local animal shelter, which is in danger of closing. It's a tough decision, because there's really no right or wrong answer. Who gets the money? Why?

What are some of the reasons you decided to act as you did? What values did you use to help you make your decision?

Values in Girl Scouting

Read the Girl Scout Promise and Law again, which you can find in the "Girl Scout Basics" chapter. The Promise and Law are a set of values shared by all girls who belong to the Girl Scouts of the USA and the World Association of Girl Guides and Girl Scouts. Discuss with a group of friends about how the Girl Scout Promise and Law can be helpful when you are faced with making a tough decision or solving a difficult problem.

Check out the list of Girl Scout values at the right. What activities do you do as a Junior Girl Scout that show these values? Try to plan some activities this year that show each of the different values of Girl Scouting.

Keeping traditions

Being proud about being female

Respecting others

Respecting yourself

Being honest

Being involved with your community

Doing service projects

Respecting the differences in people

Being a good friend

Believing in yourself

Being a good role model

Respecting the environment

Staying fit, healthy, and safe

Being responsible

Do More

If you liked learning about your values on these pages, check out the "It's Important to Me" badge in your *Junior Girl Scout Badge Book.*

It's Important to Me

Dealing with Feelings

You might be finding that every day brings lots of highs and lows—more than you ever had in the past. One minute you are feeling pretty great, and then, BAM! something happens that puts you right down in the dumps. Those ever-changing feelings are normal. And you can learn how to deal with them.

Feeling Great!

Feelings such as happiness, joy, excitement, and pride are fun to share with others. Who do you like to share your happiness with? Who is the first person you run to or call when something great happens: family, friends, your Girl Scout sisters? Maybe a teacher or a relative who lives far away?

What do you do when something bad or sad happens? Who do you go to then? The same person? People sometimes try to hide their sad feelings from others. But in many cases, letting your feelings out will help you feel better.

It's hard to talk about certain things, especially when you are upset. But those caring people you ran to when you were happy are probably also good to go to when you are blue. When you are unhappy, sometimes it's hard to figure out how to stop being unhappy. Think of caring, trusting adults you can talk to when you are feeling upset.

To start a conversation with someone about how bad you are feeling, you could say: "I need to talk to you about something that's bothering me" or "I need some advice" or "I feel really angry (or worried, or sad) and I don't know what to do."

Anger

When was the last time you were really angry? Last week? This morning? Now?

Everyone gets angry. Sometimes getting angry can be scary because you feel like you have lost control. What can you do? Lots of things! Take a walk, play a sport, talk about it, or do something you enjoy, such as a favorite hobby. Later, when you have cooled down, think about why you got angry. Try to figure out what you can do to avoid feeling angry again when you are faced with a similar situation.

Fear

What do you think girls your age are afraid of? Not being popular? Having something bad happen to their family or friends? Being picked on by a bully? Not doing well in school? Do these fears sound familiar? Do you have other fears?

One way to deal with your fears is to face them. That means you really have to think about the fear and see if it is real or not. For example, let's say you are afraid of doing badly in school. But when you think about it—or talk it over with a parent or close friend—you realize that you do pretty well in all your classes. In other words, you have probably wasted a lot of energy on a fear that wasn't even real!

Sadness

Sad things happen to everyone. Lots of things can make you feel sad: the death of a family member or a pet, your parents' divorce, moving away from your hometown, losing an important game, failing a test, or having a fight with a friend. No matter what it is that makes you feel sad, you should never feel ashamed about it.

What do you do when you are sad? Some people cry; others don't. When you cry, you are actually letting out some of the sadness inside you. Crying makes some people feel better. Some people like to be alone for awhile when they're sad. But one of the best ways to deal with sadness is by talking about it with someone you trust. Sharing your feelings is the best way to start feeling better.

Read More

For more help with feelings, read about stress management in the "Be Healthy, Be Fit" chapter of this handbook. Or help yourself relax by trying a hobby from the "Create and Invent" chapter, or a sports activity from "Be Healthy, Be Fit." Or earn the Stress Less badge from your *Junior Girl Scout Badge Book.*

Stress Less

Who Are You on the Outside?

Have you started to hear grown-ups you haven't seen in awhile tell you, "You've gotten so big?" Have you put on a favorite pair of pants lately, only to find that they end high above your ankles? Does your hair seem oilier and harder to manage? Have you gotten a pimple—or two?

If you said yes to any of these questions, you might be going through a period of life called puberty. You might start to see changes at age 8 or you may not notice anything until you are as old as 15.

Questions and Answers

The Girl Scouts has information about the body changes that happen to you during puberty in an Issues for Girl Scouts book called *Girls Are Great* that has advice, tips, and activities to help you through the sometimes awkward, sometimes confusing changes of puberty. You can get this book through your local Girl Scout council. Or, ask your troop leader for help. You can also log on to the Girl Scout Web site www.girlscouts.org and look for advice. Go to "Just for Girls" and look at the questions and answers in the "Ask Dr. M" column. Lots of girls have sent her e-mail, so you might find the answer to your question there. Look at the index to find the topic you want to know more about and click.

You can also talk with an adult you trust: a parent, older sister, teacher, school nurse, Girl Scout leader, or adult friend. Most public and school libraries have advice books you can borrow.

Here's an important thing to remember: While you might talk to your friends about the changes each of you are going through, they—like you—might not have all the facts. Make sure the information you are getting comes from a source that is reliable and accurate!

Caring for *Your Body*

The changes going on inside and outside your body are a bit like a runaway train—they can't be stopped! But by starting to take extra special care of yourself, you can get through these changes without crashing!

Your Skin

As you grow and become more active, a regular shower or bath and shampoo routine should become more important than ever. Your skin and hair might be getting oilier. That's because your sweat glands are becoming more active. Because bacteria grows in sweat, it can cause it to have a smell. You might want to start using a deodorant or antiperspirant (which decreases the amount you sweat) under your arms each day. You might want to ask an adult for help selecting one that's right for you.

You can pick up germs from lots of places. To kill germs, always wash your hands in warm water with soap for at least 20 seconds after you have used the bathroom, before you eat, and before and after you have handled food. Scrub on both sides of your hands. And don't forget to wash between your fingers and under your nails!

← Clean Hands

SOAP

CARING FOR *Your Body*

Your Face

Washing your face not only keeps you looking clean, but it gets rid of extra oil, dirt, and bacteria that can cause pimples.

Pimples are a fact of life for most kids when they enter puberty. They might find their skin becoming oily, and they might get pimples and blackheads. When the oil glands in your skin get swollen and blocked, your skin might break out. A dermatologist—skin doctor—has medicines and tips that can help you control your acne. Some things to remember: Try to keep your hair and hands off your face. If you do get a pimple, don't pick or squeeze it because if you do it can leave a scar on your face.

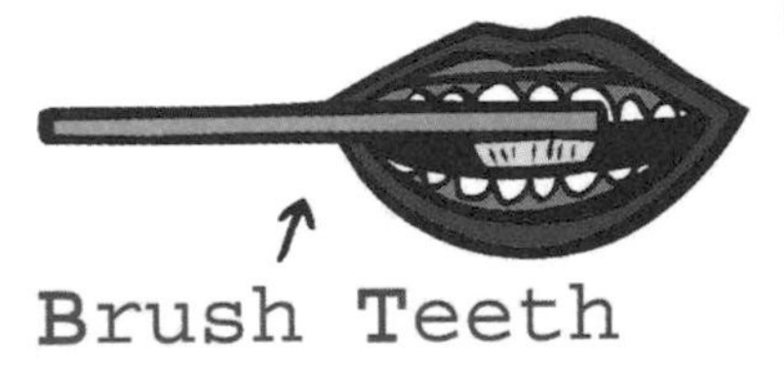

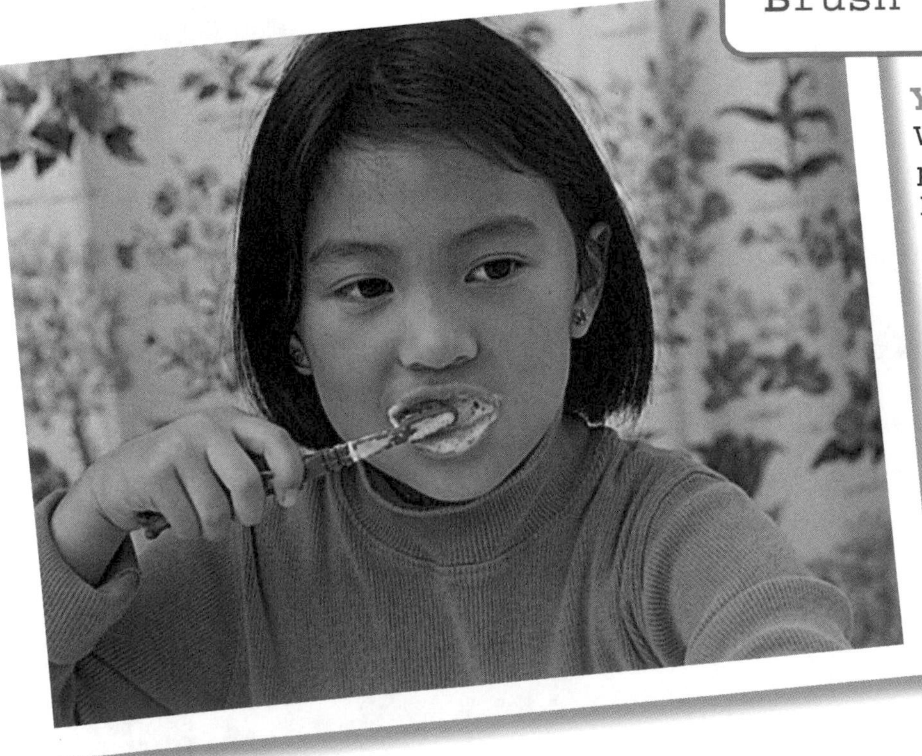

Your Teeth

When you smile, you want people to notice your clean, healthy teeth. To keep your teeth healthy, remember these tips:

- Brush after meals (or at least two times a day).
- Use dental floss, because a toothbrush can't clean *between* your teeth.
- Be especially good about brushing if you have braces.
- If you can't brush your teeth after a meal, chewing sugarless gum can help. When you chew, your mouth produces saliva, which helps clean away the bacteria.

Sun Safety

Protecting your skin from the sun is important. Even on cloudy or cold days, ultraviolet rays from the sun can damage your skin. You won't see the damage right away, but you will when you are older—wrinkles, lines, and worst of all, even skin cancer.

It's not hard to protect your skin from the sun—you just need to use a sunscreen. Sunscreens come in different degrees of protection. Use one with a rating of 15 or higher. Apply it before you go out, and reapply it frequently when you're in the sun, particularly after swimming or exercise.

Your Hair

Like your skin, your hair might be getting oilier. How often you should shampoo your hair, or use a conditioner, depends on your hair type.

There are many hair care products out there—creams, mousses, curl activators, gels, sprays, relaxers. Ask an adult to help you choose the one that is best for your type of hair. You might not even need anything more than a basic shampoo. Remember, things like blow dryers, hot combs, and curling irons can damage hair if they are used too often or used the wrong way. So be careful and check with a parent or guardian on how to care for your hair.

Do More

If the information on these pages was of interest to you, check out these badges in your *Junior Girl Scout Badge Book.*

Looking Your Best

Becoming a Teen

A Healthier You

Changing your hairstyle can give you a new look. You might want to try bangs, braids, hair bands, clips, or barrettes. Maybe you just want to part your hair differently. Remember, the best hairstyle for you is the one that suits *you*. You might feel pressured to have the same hairstyle as a friend or you might want to look like your favorite performer. But you have to decide if that hairstyle works with your type of hair or the shape of your face. Here are some different ways to braid hair.

French Braids

1. Divide the hair at the top of the head into three sections.

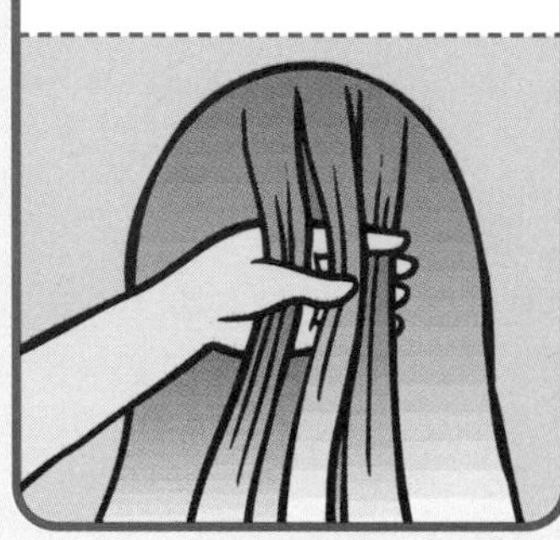

2. Cross the right section over the center section. (The center section will now be on the right.) Then take the left section and cross that over what is now the center section.

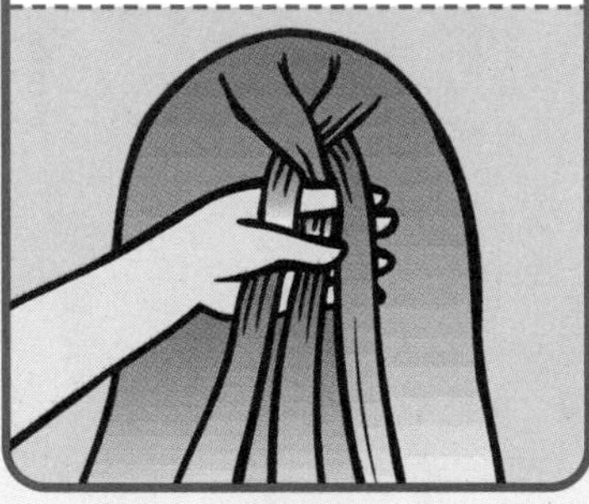

3. Take a small section of hair from the right side of the face. Add this hair to the right section of the braid.

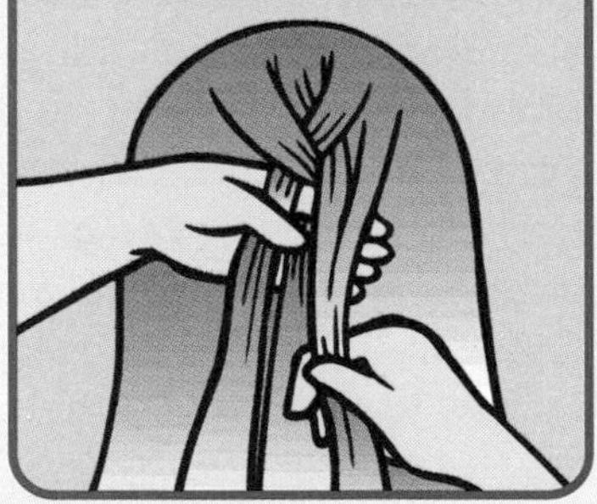

4. Cross this section over the center section.

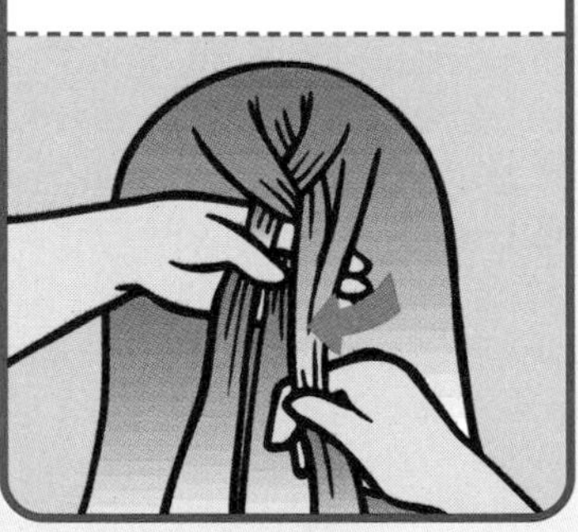

5. Hold all of the braid in your right hand and then repeat the process on the left side.

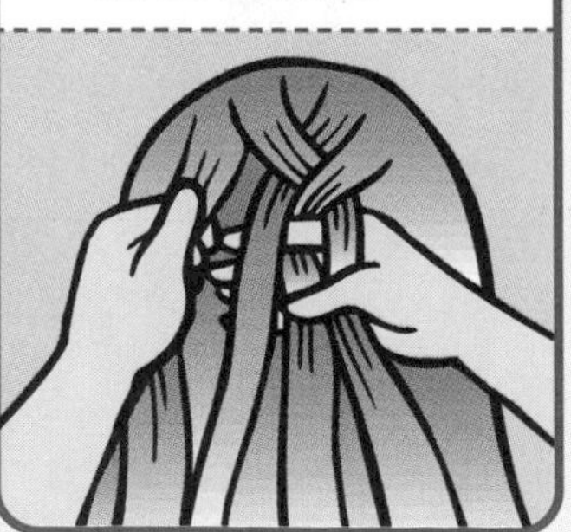

6. Continue moving from the right to the left until all the hair on either side has been caught up in the braid. Finish by braiding the bottom.

Corn Row Braids

1. Use a comb to divide a section of hair into a straight row.

2. Start making a tight braid adding hair from the right and the left and pulling to keep the braid neat and tight as you did with the French Braid, but using smaller amounts of hair within the two straight sides of the row.

3. Once you have braided all the hair in the row, secure the ends, if needed, with a band, clip, or bead.

4. Continue making rows of braids—as many as you like.

5. You can make more intricate patterns by braiding in circles or swirls.

Hair Crazy!

This particular style makes a great activity for long bus trips. You won't get bored and you will arrive looking great! Why not hold a braid workshop for other local Girl Scout troops or groups?

Hair *Wrapping*

1. Pick two colors of embroidery thread.

2. Cut double strands three times as long as your hair.

3. Make a small braid in your hair.

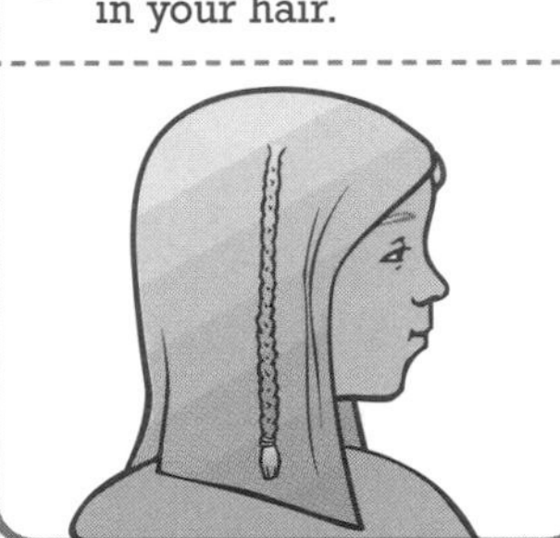

4. Tie the strands under the braid at the top.

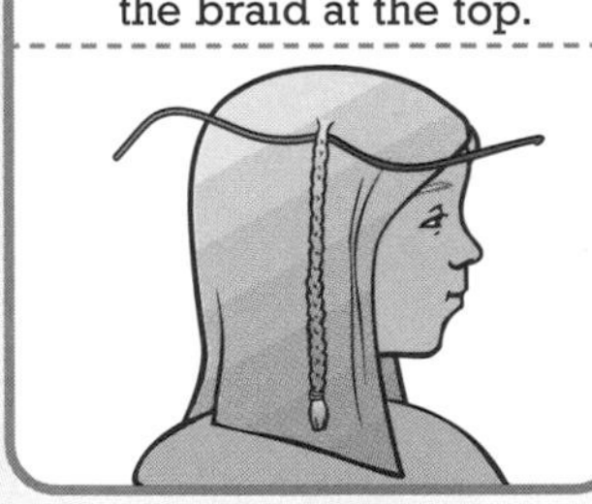

5. Hold the braid and one color together, and start twisting the other color tightly around the braid and the other color.

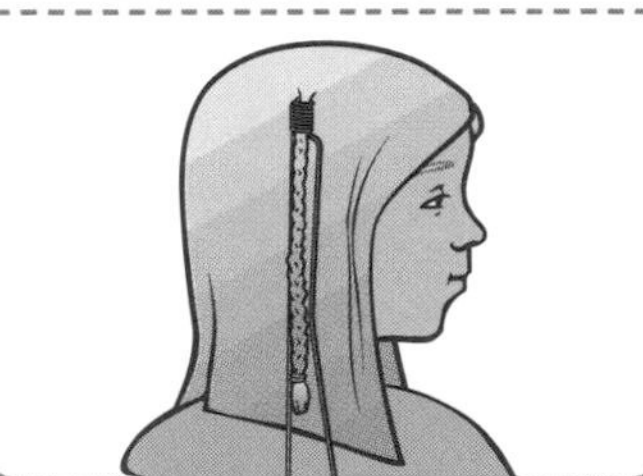

6. At some point, stop using the first color, and start twisting with the second color, making sure the strand of the first color is now under the second color.

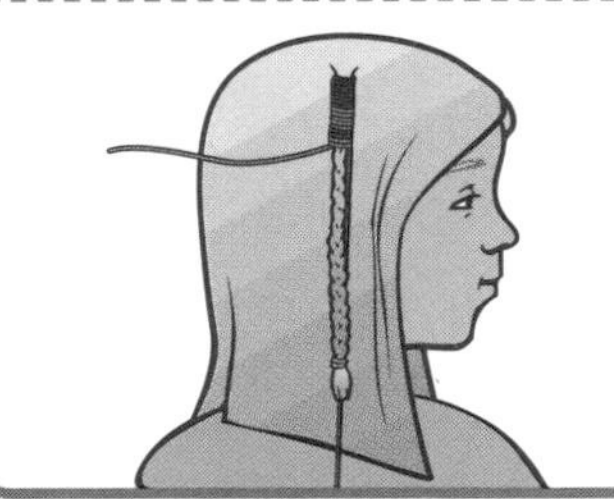

You can wrap half of the braid with one color, and half with the other. Do large or small stripes—whatever pattern you like! Try them all!

Do More

If you enjoyed these hair-styling activities, you might be interested in these badges in your *Junior Girl Scout Badge Book.*

Looking Your Best

Being My Best

Activity:

Homemade Hair Ornaments

Decorate your own barrettes and headbands with beads or ribbons.

What You Need
- Barrettes and headbands
- Things to decorate with: beads, glitter, ribbons, bows, yarn
- Fabric glue
- Liquid embroidery or fabric paint

What You Do

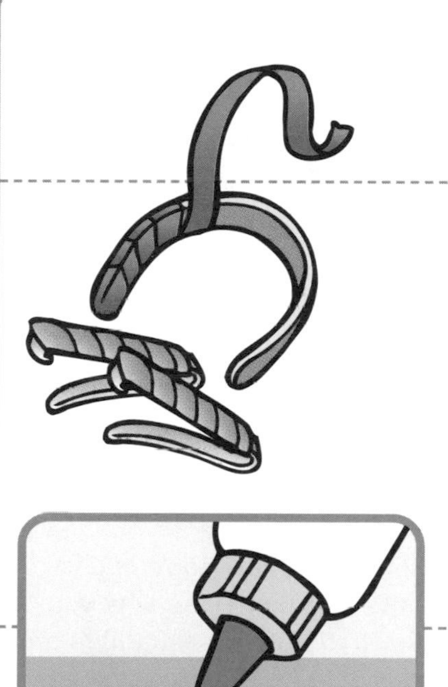

1. Take a plain headband or a barrette and wrap it with ribbons, fabric, or yarn.
2. Sew or glue on beads or bows.

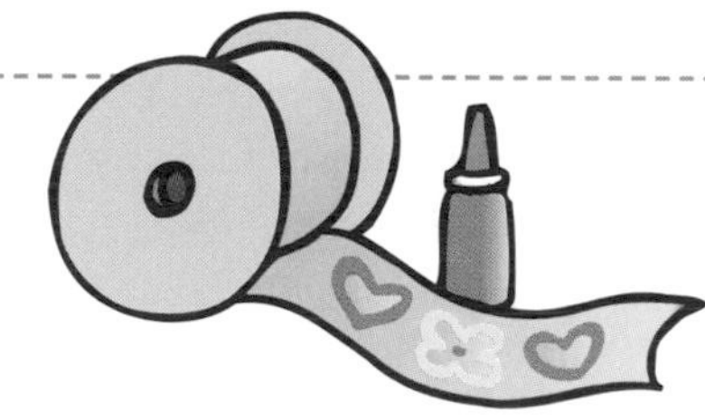

3. Use liquid embroidery or fabric paint to draw pictures or write words on the ribbon or fabric, such as the name of your Girl Scout council.

Makes a great swap!

Liking Yourself

It's Monday morning and you stretch before you get out of bed. You feel rested after a good night's sleep. You brush your teeth, comb your hair, and pull on your clothes. As you turn to grab your books, you take a quick look in the mirror and think

_______________________!

What Is Beautiful?

Some people look in a mirror and like what they see; others don't. Most girls want to look their best. Unfortunately, lots of girls believe that in order to be popular, they must be beautiful.

Feeling good about yourself is about much more than how you look. First, what is beautiful to one person might not be to another. Some girls think wavy or curly hair looks the best and others love the look of straight hair. Second, most people think real beauty includes things that you can't always see; intelligence, friendliness, and kindness, for example. Think about your best friends. Are you friends with them because of the way they look, or for other reasons?

What do you think would happen if you asked a group of Junior Girl Scouts to each give an example of a person who was beautiful? You would probably have different answers and lots of disagreement over what makes someone beautiful.

Picture Perfect

Unfortunately, what people think of as beautiful has a lot to do with what they see in magazines, on television, in movies, and in books. Think about it: Models have pimples and bad hair days just like you! They just have lots of people working behind the scenes to make sure that what you see is "perfect." There are people who do their makeup, design the best lighting for their faces, and touch up their photos to make them look better.

Weight Check

Some girls believe that in order to be "beautiful" they have to look like a model or an actress.

They might look in the mirror and see themselves as "fat" or "overweight" when they aren't at all. They go on diets to become even thinner or exercise more than what is considered normal or healthy. Being very underweight can be dangerous to your health. On the other hand, some girls really are overweight and that isn't healthy either. Always check with a doctor or nurse to find out what weight is right for your body type. These professionals can help you figure out safe, healthy ways to lose or gain weight, if it's necessary.

Remember, most people can't look like models. And that's okay!

Do More

If this section was of interest to you, check out these badges in your *Junior Girl Scout Badge Book.*

Consumer Power

Being My Best

Communication

The Choice Is Yours

Are Ads Real?

Do you believe the ads you see on TV or in magazines? The people who make the ads sure hope you do! Think about what makes you buy something like clothes or CDs or even school supplies. You probably make a lot of choices based on the ads you see. Even if you feel you don't pay much attention to commercials or ads, you sometimes can't help but remember them. Sometimes commercials use jingles (catchy songs) or phrases that just stick in your head.

Advertisers try to convince you of lots of things. They might want you to think that a product is safe for the environment, good for your health, or fun to use, eat, or drink. They want you to believe that you will be more popular, attractive, successful, happy, or rich if you buy the product. But what product can do all those things?

Next time you are looking at a commercial or ad, ask yourself: Can the product really do all of the things it says it can? Maybe the ad doesn't even *say* it can do something, but the advertiser uses pretty people, catchy music, or other positive messages to make you think it's a great product.

Activity:

Media Magic

Find out what magazine editors think is beautiful.

What You Need

- Lots of different types of magazines (sports, gardening, women's, teen, etc.)
- Scissors
- Paper
- Glue or glue stick

What You Do

1. Look through the pages. Clip out at least a dozen photos of women, girls, and men from each magazine. The photos can be from advertisements, or from articles.
2. Make a collage of the photos for each type of magazine.
3. Compare what images represent beauty in each magazine. Are there differences between the magazines?
4. Bring your collages to a Girl Scout meeting. Ask your troop to talk about what the magazines use to show beauty. Discuss whether you feel this is realistic. Why or why not?

4 Family and Friends

In This Chapter You Will Learn About:

If you ask three of your friends to tell you why their families are important to them, you will probably get three different answers.

"We love each other and have fun together."

"My family helps me feel good about myself."

"They protect me and take care of me."

What makes a family unique? You might live with two parents or with one, or you might be cared for and loved by people who are not your parents. You might have many sisters and brothers, two, one, or none. Great-grandparents, grandparents, step-parents, foster parents, guardians, aunts, uncles, and cousins might be part of your family. They might live with you or live nearby or far away. You might see them often, or only on special occasions.

Your family will never be exactly like someone else's. And only you can describe how your family is important to you. Think about what makes your family special. Find a way to let your family know how special they are to you.

Fun Things To Do with Your Family

Do you wish you had more time to talk to your family about what's going on in your life, at school, in Girl Scouts? You and your family members might be so busy that you don't spend as much time together as you would like. If you want to have more time together, try some of these ideas:

- Pick a time every night for your family to have Special Talk Time. Or ask that everyone attend a family meeting once a week.
- Organize a family project that everyone works on, such as planting a garden, making a scrapbook for a grandparent, organizing family photos, or repainting a room.
- For the next holiday, plan special menus, decorations, and events.
- Invent new family rituals. For example, create a "Back to School" event, or a "First Day of Summer" celebration.
- Pick one night as a Special Family Fun Night. Decide together how you will spend your time: rent a movie, play a game, cook a meal together. (See the Family Fun Jar activity later in this chapter for more ideas.)
- Save family memories and stories. Make sure that photographs, family videos and movies, souvenirs, awards, letters and cards, artwork, and projects are kept and displayed. Interview family members so you can create your own family history.
- Do something together: volunteer work, camping,a sport, a vacation, or work in a community organization.
- Work together on Girl Scout activities. Are you practicing your camping skills? Ask a family member to help. Are you working on a service project? Ask family members to join you. Are you learning a new craft or sports move? Ask a family member to try it with you.

Year-Round Family Fun

Try one or more activities from these pages. Or try all of them! You might have such a good time that you and your family invent some new kinds of fun and games. If you do, be sure to share them with your Girl Scout friends!

The Sun Is Shining—Head Outdoors

- Take a walk but pretend you have just moved into your neighborhood. What do you see when you are looking at familiar things with "new" eyes?

- Help the adults in your family relive their childhoods! Ask them to teach you the outdoor games they played when they were your age, such as Tag, Red Rover, Kick the Can, or Duck, Duck, Goose. Do these games make them act like kids again?

- Plan an all-day trip to a favorite spot, or to someplace new. Pack a picnic lunch. Brings lots of water and some high-energy snack foods to keep the group moving along.

- Put your home repair skills into action by repairing something around your home. Then help out a neighbor who may not have the skills or money to do a necessary repair.

The Rain Is Falling—Stay Inside

- Plan an indoor picnic. Make picnic foods together, set up a picnic blanket, and play some board or card games.

- Create an indoor bowling alley with empty plastic bottles and a small ball. You can use different sizes of bottles (smaller bottles can equal more points) to make the game more interesting. Pick teams or compete individually.

- Organize family photos. You can create photo file boxes or scrapbooks by theme: sports, birthdays, baby photos, holidays. Decide as a group which photos are worth saving. Together, enjoy your newly organized collection.

- Cook a family-style meal in which each person adds a dish or an ingredient. You can make a soup or a stew—every person gets a vegetable to peel or cut up. You can plan a more elaborate meal. You can draw placemats, fold napkins into special shapes, light some candles, create a centerpiece, and/or take turns playing waiter.

- Use a lamp without a shade and some paper tacked onto a wall to cast each family member's silhouette onto the paper. Trace, color, and cut out each silhouette, and then create a silhouette grouping of your family.

- Homemade congratulations cards are wonderful pick-me-ups. Write down the name of each family member on a piece of paper, fold, and put inside a bag. Take turns pulling out a name. (If you get your own, put it back in and try again.) Then with paper and pen, crayons, paints, or your computer, create a congratulations card to celebrate a recent accomplishment by that family member.

Activity:

Family Fun Jar

Use a clean jar or other container as a Family Fun Jar. Decorate your container with symbols or photos of the fun your family has had together on trips, or doing hobbies or other family activities. On separate pieces of paper, write down things you can do together, such as:

Play a board game.

Go out for ice cream.

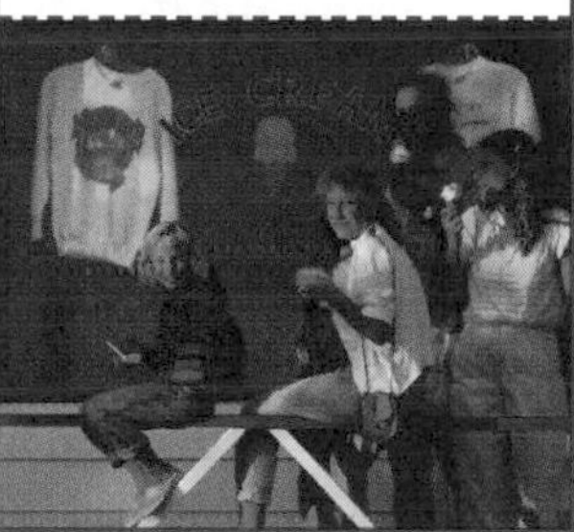

Get out the video camera and shoot some film.

Ask the adults to tell stories about their childhoods.

Go for a bike ride.

Take a walk around the neighborhood.

Choose a special time each week—or more often if everyone can make it—to go to the Family Fun Jar, pick out an activity, and do it together.

Family Rules

Every family has its own set of rules, and each family member has to do certain jobs around the house. Your family's rules about TV-watching, bedtimes, chores, and homework might be very different from your friends' family rules. Maybe you think that your family's rules are too strict. Or that they're not strict enough. You might think that some of your family's rules are not fair, especially about who does what chores. Members of a family need to work together to resolve their problems.

How Do You Ask for Change?

1. Write down the chores that each member of your family now does. If you don't think the chores are divided fairly, prepare a new list and talk to your family about why you think the chores should be divided up that way.

2. If you are not happy about your family's rules, set a time for a meeting to discuss them. Think carefully about your issues before the meeting so that you can express your ideas clearly.

It's Not Always Easy

Big and little problems happen in every family. You can watch TV families solve their problems, even very serious ones, in one hour or less. That's not very realistic. Sometimes unhappy things happen, such as divorce, and you can do nothing about it. But in some situations there *are* ways to ease a sticky problem.

Are you fighting a lot with a brother or sister? Try using the tips in this section to help you talk to each other. If your family cannot agree on something, check out the ideas about how to work with groups in the "Adventures in Girl Scouting" chapter. No matter what, find a time and place to talk with your family when you need to. Being able to talk to each other is what helps keep families close.

Communication

One of the most important skills you can work on is your ability to communicate. Why is this skill so important? There are many reasons:

- If you want to convince your parents to increase your allowance money, you need to communicate why this is important to you.
- If you want your best friend to return things that she's borrowed, you need to remind her, in a gentle but clear manner.
- If you find yourself misunderstanding the assignments in science class, you need to improve your listening skills and learn how to ask your teacher the right questions.

All of these situations require you to be able to communicate well. Talking and listening—that's communication.

Test Yourself: *Are You a Good Listener?*

Look at the differences between a good listener and a bad listener. Which are you?

Good listener: Pays attention to the person who is talking. Makes eye contact.
Bad listener: Doesn't pay attention. Often looks away.

Good listener: Concentrates on what the other person is saying.
Bad listener: Thinks more about herself than what the other person is saying.

Good listener: Doesn't interrupt and doesn't think about how she will answer until after the other person is finished talking.
Bad listener: Interrupts often, plans an answer before the other person is finished talking.

Good listener: Asks questions to help her understand what she heard.
Bad listener: Doesn't bother to make sure she understands things correctly.

Learn to Speak Out

Suppose you and your family are trying to decide on a video to rent. Your brother suggests getting a horror movie and the others agree. But you hate horror movies. You say, "I really don't like horror movies. How about seeing a comedy or action movie instead?"

You have let your family know how you feel and you have given everyone a few choices. You responded *assertively,* which means you expressed yourself honestly and stood up for yourself while at the same time showing respect for the rights and feelings of others.

What if you had said, "I'm not going to watch THAT kind of movie and if you rent it I'm going to go to my room instead!" Like the response above, you let people know that you wanted to see another movie. But do you think your family liked the way you said it? Probably not. In this case, you responded *aggressively*. You didn't show respect for others, which will make it hard for them to respond to you in a positive way.

There is another way you could have handled the situation. You could have gone along with the others without saying anything at all. That would have been a *passive* response, which means you allowed others to make a decision for you.

Test Yourself: *What Would You Say?*

What would be the assertive way to handle each of these situations? What is the aggressive approach? What is the passive response?

- **You have been waiting on line 30 minutes to buy tickets to a movie. Suddenly, a boy your age jumps in line ahead of you. This might prevent you from getting a ticket. Would you go tell a grown-up? Shrug your shoulders and hope you still get a seat? Yell at him to go to the back of the line? Would you respond differently if a person your parents' age cut in front of you? What would you say in that case?**
- **Your mom tells you to clean up your room. You said you would be at your friend's apartment in five minutes and besides, it was your sister who made the mess. Would you try to tell your mom the truth? Would you leave anyway, because it wasn't your mess? Would you find your sister and make her clean it up? Would you clean it up yourself?**
- **One of the girls in your class—a really big bully—takes your pencil off your desk for the fourth time today, chews the eraser, and then throws it back to you. Would you dump her books on the floor? Speak to your teacher? Be upset, but do nothing?**

Do More

If you enjoyed learning about communication skills, or are interested in developing good relationships with family and friends, check out these badges in your *Junior Girl Scout Badge Book.*

Healthy Relationships

Across Generations

Communication

Friends for Life

Junior Girl Scouts is a great place to be when it comes to having friendships with a capital "F." You not only get to do great stuff with friends you already have, but you also get to make lots of new friends—in your neighborhood, in your community, even internationally.

Do I Have Enough Friends?

There are no rules about how many friends a person should have. Some girls have many, some a few, and others have one. If you are happy with yourself, you will find it easy to make and keep friends. People like being around people who are positive and enthusiastic.

How Friendships Change

Some friendships will stay with you during your entire life. Others will change, or even end, as your interests and experiences change. For example, if you join the swim team, you might spend a lot of time at practice improving your skills. You will probably start to hang out with other kids who are into swimming as much as you are. You might introduce your new swim-team friends to your old friends and find out that everyone gets along. You might do some things with your new friends and other things with your old friends. That's a normal part of growing up.

Finding New Friends

In addition to the friends you will make in Girl Scouts, you can also meet new friends by joining a club, sports team, or an activity group at school.

Test Yourself: *What Kind of Friend Are You?*

Drop that "r" out of friend—the "R" for Respect, Real, Relate, and Rescue—and you get fiend (an evil monster). Are you a friend or a fiend? Pick one answer for each question.

1 My friend comes running with BIG news she can't wait to tell me.

- ☐ A I drop everything, listen, and let her know I am happy for her.
- ☐ B I listen to her for a second and then tell her MY big news.
- ☐ C I look away from the TV long enough to say, "I only get to watch this show once a day!"

2 I found out that a friend blurted out something I had sworn her to keep secret.

- ☐ A I find time when we can be alone and ask her to tell me why she did it.
- ☐ B I freeze her out for at least a month.
- ☐ C I tell all of her secrets to every kid in school.

3 My friend and I have gotten into a routine: every Friday night we rent a video and take turns sleeping over. My friend tells me she can't make it this Friday.

- ☐ A I call my cousin, whom I haven't seen in ages, and make plans with her.
- ☐ B I feel disappointed and jealous. I should come first.
- ☐ C I make plans without her every Friday for the next year!

4 When my friend and I decide what we want to do:

- ☐ A We usually take turns doing what she wants and what I want.
- ☐ B I feel like she gets her way a lot more than I do.
- ☐ C It's my way or the highway!

5 If I overhear a group at school saying bad things about my friend,

- ☐ A I interrupt and defend her.
- ☐ B I keep quiet because I don't want them talking about me.
- ☐ C I join in since I have even more dirt to contribute!

Count up which letter you picked most.

Mostly **A**—You have great friendship skills.

Mostly **B**—You need to work harder on being a good friend.

Mostly **C**—Do you have any friends? You need to start being a good friend while you have some left!

It's PARTY Time!

Plan a party to celebrate your friendships. Or throw a party so you can get to know people better. You can have a party at home, in a park, in a backyard, at a skating rink, or some other place where people gather. A party can be small, with just one or two friends. Or it can be large, with many family members and Girl Scout friends.

Party Activities
If you look through this book, you can find a lot of activities that are fun to do at a party. Pick a game or a craft activity or plan a party around earning a badge.

Party Planning
Have you ever gone to a party that was a great success? What in particular made it fun? With your Girl Scout troop or group, think of what makes a party fun both for the people who are giving the party (hosts) and for people who are attending the party (guests). The worksheet below will help you plan.

Party Theme ___________

Place ___________________

Guests __________________

Refreshments/Food _______

Activities _______________

Other ________________

Party Popcorn
Popcorn is an easy party food to make and almost everybody likes it. You can use plain, already-popped popcorn from the store, or pop it on the stove following directions on the can, or pop some in the microwave. Make your plain popcorn into festive party popcorn with these additions:

Cinnamon Sugar
Mix ½ cup of plain white sugar with 1 teaspoon of cinnamon and sprinkle over a large bowl of plain popcorn.*

Peanut Pop
Mix a can of roasted peanuts or flavored peanuts into a large bowl of plain popcorn.

Cheese Popcorn
Mix ½ cup of grated cheese into a large bowl of popcorn.*

Chocolate Chip Popcorn
Mix 1 cup of chocolate chips (the kind you use to make cookies) into a large bowl of plain popcorn.*

* See page 208 for the metric conversion chart.

Activity:

Fly a Flag of Friendship

Try this activity that celebrates you and your friends.

What You Need

- Large piece of plain fabric or felt
- Smaller pieces of plain fabric or felt—about the size of this book
- Fabric paint, pencils, or markers
- Glitter, sequins, colorful buttons
- White glue
- Colorful cord or twine

What You Do

1. Each girl takes her piece of fabric and decorates it in a way that shows her interests, talents, and activities. For example, a girl who is into soccer might draw a soccer ball. A girl who loves to play the piano might glue on a mini-piano made of felt. You could also use photos of yourself doing your favorite activities.
2. When all the banners are done, lay them face side down and run some glue along the back top edge.
3. Lay the cord or twine along the line of glue and press it down so that it sticks.
4. Let the glue dry.

The Peer Pressure Cooker

Have you ever done or said something because your friends were doing it? Did you do it mainly to keep your friends or because you wanted to stay in a group? That's peer pressure. Lots of girls your age feel pressured by their peers. Your peers can be girls in Girl Scouts, your classmates, other friends, or even kids you don't know. Often peer pressure makes you feel like you have to act a certain way, look a certain way, or have only certain friends in order to "fit in."

Peer Pressure Can Be Good or Bad

GOOD: When it helps you feel good about yourself and you are learning new skills. Example: Two friends pressured you into presenting your service project idea to your troop. Although you were nervous, your presentation went well and you felt good about all your hard work.

BAD: When it makes you feel uncomfortable, confused, or gets you in trouble. Example: Your friends convince you to use all the allowance you've saved to buy trading cards instead of saving some of it, as you had promised your parents you would.

Why Do People Pressure Others?

Some people like to control other people. Some think it makes them more popular. Others do it so they can feel important.

How to Deal with Peer Pressure

1. **Stand up for yourself!** Don't let others lead you to do something you would be ashamed of later.

2. **Speak your mind.** Tell people how you really feel. They might learn something from you.

3. **Respect the feelings and decisions of others.** Let others follow their own decisions. You follow yours.

4. **Find support from others.** If you feel pressured in a bad way, talk to someone you trust.

5. **Stay away** from or ignore the group, if necessary.

Are You Hanging with the Right Crowd?

To help you decide whether a group of friends is right for you, ask yourself these questions:

- Do I feel comfortable with them?
- Do they accept me for who I am?
- Are their values the same as mine?
- Do they make me happy most of the time?
- Do they make me feel good about myself?
- Do I want others, including my family, to know I'm part of this group?

If you have answered yes to most of these questions, this group is probably right for you.

What's a Clique?

A clique is a group of people who hang out only with other members of the group and ignore people who aren't in their group.

Being friends with people who share the same interests with you is not the same as being in a clique.

What are the warning signs that tell you if you and your friends are in a clique?

- You don't let anyone else in the group and think you are better than other people.
- You ignore kids who are different from you.
- You often tease or make fun of other kids.
- You are mean to members who want to get out of the clique.
- You aren't interested in meeting new people or trying new things.

Test Yourself: *What Would You Do?*

There are no right and wrong answers to this test. Think about how you would react if any of these things happened to you. Then think about someone you admire—maybe an older sister, your grandmother, a religious group leader. How do you think she or he would react in the same situation?

- A classmate asks you to cheat on a test. What would you do?
- Your girlfriend's sister offers you a sip of beer. Would you try it?
- Everyone is wearing designer jeans and your father says it's silly to spend that amount of money on clothes. Would you find a way to earn the money and buy the jeans anyway?
- Your stepmother buys you a great outfit. You really like it, but your friends say it is ugly. Would you wear it again?
- Your parents always expect you to come home early. Your friends make fun of you and call you a baby. What do you tell them?

Dealing with Bullies

Every afternoon for the last two weeks, Damaris has followed Michelle home from school. Damaris calls her names, tries to get her to fight, and takes money from her. Michelle is afraid to tell her grandmother because she doesn't want Damaris to find out she told anyone.

Damaris is a bully. Picking on others makes a bully feel powerful. Bullies shove, punch, steal from, make fun of, fight, or pick on others. Sometimes bullies are not that obvious; they spread false rumors, freeze out other kids, or lie about what you have said. In those cases, the innocent victim usually does not have a clue about what is going on.

How to Stop a Bully

1. Get your friends to help by standing up for you.

2. Ignore the bully or avoid the bully.

3. Run away from the bully.

4. Stand up to the bully and tell her or him to stop.

5. Get an adult to help you. Talk to a teacher or school official, to a family member, or to your Girl Scout leader or another trusted adult. If you think that the bully might be dangerous and could physically hurt you or others, you need to talk to an adult as soon as possible.

6. If your school doesn't have a program to stop bullies, start one with other kids and adults. Research anti-bully programs at other schools for ideas about how to make yours work.

The Problem with Name-calling

Besides being very hurtful, name-calling can lead others to form stereotypes. Stereotyping means grouping people into categories because of one small thing you might know or think you know about them. This is an unfair way of looking at people because you never really get to know the individual.

Read the story at the right. Kids who don't know Maria and heard what Kathy said might think Maria is klutzy, or not too bright, and might never ask her to be a part of a school project or sports team. And they might put her close friends in the same category, believing them all to be "losers."

The next time you hear name-calling, what could you say or do to stop it?

Words Can Sometimes Hurt

Maria balanced her lunch tray—her pizza, milk, and apple were sliding around—as she looked for someplace to sit. She saw Allison sitting with her usual lunch group. Maria and Allison had been paired up in gym class and Allison seemed nice.

"Is it okay if I sit here?" Maria asked quietly.

"Ummm, sure," said Allison without looking up.

Maria started to sit down on the bench between Allison and Kathy. She heard someone giggle at the other end of the table.

"Would anybody like to play baseball after school today?" asked Kathy.

"I would," said Allison. **"Maria, would you like to come?"**

Maria quickly looked up just as she was setting her tray down. **"I would love. . . ."** Splat! Her pizza slid right off the plate into Kathy's lap.

"I'm sorry, Kathy . . . it was an accident . . . I didn't mean. . . ."

Kathy started screaming before Maria could even finish. **"Oh, Maria! You're such a jerk! How could you be so clumsy? Forget it—you're not playing baseball with us today. You're such a loser!"**

How would you feel if you were Maria? If you were Allison, what would you say to Maria? To Kathy?

Pretend you are sitting at the other end of this lunch table and have witnessed this event. You are friends with both Maria and Kathy and are looking forward to the baseball game after school. Continue the story, describing how you would stop your friends from fighting.

Fight Prejudice and Discrimination

As you meet more people, you will get to know people who are different from yourself. They might have different religious beliefs, come from different countries, or have a disability, such as blindness, deafness, or an inability to walk.

You might also meet people who are prejudiced, which means that they have a negative feeling or opinion about a person because of her race, background, religion, disability, or other difference. When someone acts unfairly toward another person because of prejudice, that's called discrimination.

Sometimes you might read things on Web sites or see things on television that make fun of or say bad things about certain groups of people. When you hear or read things like this, it can be very hard to speak out against it or to defend the person who is being picked on. But as a Girl Scout, you have made a promise to respect others and be a sister to all Girl Scouts, who come from many different backgrounds.

Ideas for Busting Prejudice

1. When you hear people saying unfair things, tell them that you don't want to listen. Tell them that people who respect themselves also respect others.

2. Work on a project that brings together people of many different backgrounds. Working together towards a common goal helps people understand more about each other.

People with Disabilities

Sarah is blind and reads by using Braille, a special type of printing in which raised dots are felt by the fingers. Sarah sings in chorus, loves to solve math problems, and has a cool tool that enables her to write e-mail to friends on the Web.

Naoko uses crutches to get around. She writes stories, enjoys belting out the words to favorite songs with her friends, and is the team manager of her school's basketball team.

Girl Scouts with and without disabilities have worked together since 1912 to learn camping skills, do service projects, and complete badge requirements.

Sign Language

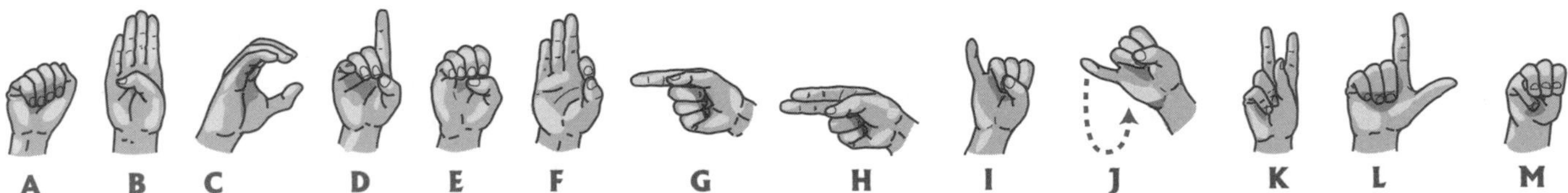

5 How to Stay Safe

In This Chapter You Will Learn About:

How to Make a Difference

What are you going to do to beat out prejudice and discrimination in your community? Here are some ideas:

- Do a survey of your meeting place to find out how accessible it is for people with disabilities. Measure the doorways and bathroom facilities to figure out if someone in a wheelchair would be able to get through. Think of ways to get rid of any obstacles.
- Study the finger-spelling sign language alphabet below. Learn to sign your name and say "hello," "I am a Girl Scout," "please," "thank you," and "goodbye."
- Write a "contract" that makes certain behavior unacceptable. For example, "No jokes that make fun of people. If I hear one, I'll tell the person to stop." Get at least three people to sign the contract.
- Plan a "Prejudice-Free Day" in your community or school. Use the action-plan steps in the "Adventures in Girl Scouting" chapter to help you get started.

There are a lot of things you can do to fight discrimination. You have the power to make changes. You have the power to help people learn to live and work together. It starts with you.

What are some of your ideas?

____

____

____

____

____

____

____

Do More

Check out the activities in your *Junior Girl Scout Badge Book* that celebrate people's differences, such as:

Celebrating People

Humans and Habitats

Globe Trotting

Global Awareness

World Neighbors

My Community

My Heritage

N

O

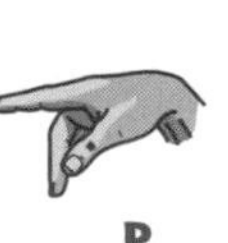
P

Q

R

S

T

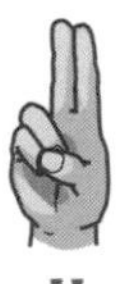
U

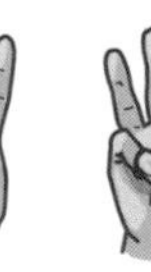
V

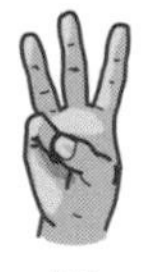
W

X

Y

Z

GIRL SCOUT FIRST AID KIT

One of the best reasons to stay safe and healthy is that it will enable you to do all the fun, wonderful things Girl Scouting has to offer. Whether you are at home, at the park, at a friend's house, or walking down the street, you need to know some basic safety skills. In this chapter, you will find lots of tips, facts, and activities on topics such as first aid, personal safety, and making healthy choices.

Emergency Telephone Calling
Practice making emergency telephone calls (do not actually call) with your troop or group or with an adult. Learn how to give the most important information (your name, where you are, what happened) quickly and how to follow the directions given to you. Here are some role-playing situations:

- You see smoke coming out of the apartment building next door.
- Your friend accidentally drank some gasoline that was stored in a soda bottle.
- You are home alone and you hear glass breaking downstairs.
- The lights suddenly go out in your house.

Emergency Phone List

Keep an up-to-date list of emergency telephone numbers near every phone in your home. It should look something like this:

Work numbers for family members:

Home numbers for family members:

Neighbors:

Emergency medical services:

Police:

Fire department:

Poison control center:

Doctor:

Dentist:

Utilities:

Taxi or car service:

Other important numbers:

A Safety Game

Play this fun game with one other person. See how many basic safety rules you already know.

What You Need

- Two dice
- Two beads or coins to use as tokens

What You Do

1. Get two different beads or coins to use as tokens. Put both tokens on the Start/Finish square.
2. Roll one of the dice each turn. Players move around the game board in opposite directions. Once you land on a square, follow the instructions, if any, written on it. Then the next player rolls the dice and takes her turn.
3. The first player to reach the Start/Finish square is the winner. You don't need to roll an exact number to get to Finish. (*Note*: Start and Finish share the same square.)

The crossing guard says to wait until the light turns green before crossing the street. You run across the street while the light is yellow. **Lose a turn.** ☹

You forget to wear your seat belt. **Lose a turn.** ☹

Walking at night, you wear light or white clothing, and you follow the buddy system. Good for you! **Move forward one square.**

You take a shortcut through a dark alley. **Go back two squares.**

You carry extra change in a safe place to make an emergency call. Smart move! **Move forward one square.**

A stranger offers you candy and you take it. What were you thinking? **Lose a turn.** ☹

You think someone is following you, so you go straight to an adult you know, a police officer, or into a store. **Move forward one square.**

While at a shopping center, you don't pick a meeting place in case you get separated from your family or friends. **Go back two squares.**

When you get lost, you remain calm. **Move forward two squares.**

You always wear a helmet when you ride your bike. You're no dummy! **Move forward one square.**

Your buddy tries to convince you to play near an abandoned building, but you won't. **Move forward one square.**

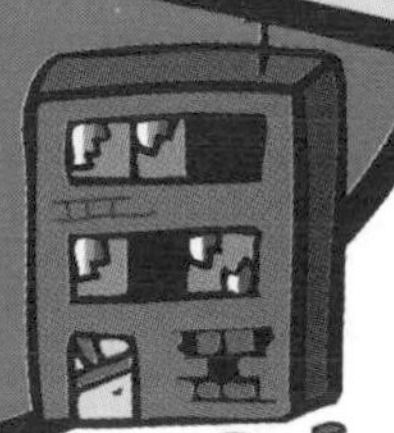

You forget to turn the television and other electrical appliances off during a lightning storm. **Lose a turn.** ☹

You instruct a group of younger children to stay away from downed power lines, loose tree branches, and deep puddles after a storm. **Move forward one square.**

First Aid

First aid is the care you give someone who is hurt or ill before medical help arrives.

When an accident or emergency happens:

1. Stay calm.
2. Get an adult to help you.
3. Call a doctor or the local emergency assistance number (9-1-1 in many places) if the injury is serious.
4. Wear latex gloves to protect yourself from blood or other bodily fluids.
5. Do not move an injured person unless there is danger, like fire or exposed electrical wires.
6. Once help arrives, tell an adult about the first aid you gave.

First Aid Kit

Be prepared. Put together a troop or family first aid kit. A list of items to include are on the next page.

Do More

If you're interested in this topic, check out the "First Aid" badge in the *Junior Girl Scout Badge Book.*

First Aid

- ☐ First aid book
- ☐ Soap
- ☐ Safety pins
- ☐ Scissors
- ☐ Distilled (not tap) water in an unbreakable container
- ☐ Tweezers
- ☐ Sewing needle
- ☐ Matches
- ☐ Adhesive tape and bandages
- ☐ Flashlight
- ☐ Paper drinking cups
- ☐ Sterile gauze
- ☐ Triangular bandage or clean cloth
- ☐ Cotton swabs
- ☐ Oral thermometer
- ☐ Non-latex gloves
- ☐ Instant chemical ice pack
- ☐ Pocket face-shield
- ☐ Plastic bag
- ☐ Emergency telephone numbers
- ☐ Change for telephone call

First Aid Guide

Here are solutions to common problems that can affect the safety and health of anyone you know.

Animal Bite

Wash the wound with soap and warm water. Apply a sterile bandage or cloth. Call a doctor. Try to identify the animal in case it needs to be tested for rabies.

Bleeding

Important: Latex gloves must be worn when caring for bleeding wounds.

- Small cuts: Clean the cut with soap and warm water, and cover with a bandage.
- Large cuts that are bleeding a lot: Put a clean cloth directly on the wound and press firmly until the bleeding stops. Use adhesive tape to hold the cloth in place. Raise the bleeding part above the level of the person's heart if possible. Call a doctor, a hospital, or your local emergency assistance number.

Blisters

Wash the area with soap and warm water. Cover with a clean bandage. Do not break the blister.

Bumps and Bruises

Put a cold, damp cloth on the area. If there is a lot of swelling, call an adult for help.

Burns

If the burn has not broken or charred the skin, place the burned area in cold (not ice) water, pat dry, and cover with a dry, sterile cloth. Do NOT use ointment, butter, or petroleum jelly. Have an adult check the burn. If the skin is broken, blistered, or charred, call a doctor, hospital, or local emergency assistance number.

Choking

See opposite page.

Drowning

Call the lifeguard or go for help immediately. Do not go into the water yourself to get someone out. Find an adult to do Cardio-Pulmonary Resuscitation (CPR) and rescue breathing.

Eye Injuries

When a person gets hit in the eye, put a cold, clean cloth over it. Have the eye checked by a doctor.

- Small objects: If small objects (like an eyelash or piece of dirt) get into the eye, do not let the person rub her eye. Have the person bend so that her head is sideways. Pour a cup of cool water over the opened eye. Have the person move her eyeball up and down. If an object is sticking into the eyeball, don't try to remove it. Call the doctor, hospital, or local emergency assistance number.

- Chemical burns: If bleach or some other cleaning chemical gets into the eye, turn the person's head to the side so that the eye with the chemical burn is on the bottom. Let water from a faucet or cup run slowly across the eye from the part closest to the nose. Rinse the eye for at least 15 minutes. Cover the eye with a clean, dry cloth. Call a doctor, hospital, or local emergency assistance number.

Fainting

If a person feels faint (as if she can't stand up), help her lie down or bend over with her head between her knees. Loosen tight clothing. Wipe her face with cool water. If the person has fainted and doesn't open her eyes quickly, call the doctor, hospital, or local emergency assistance number.

Choking

If the person can speak, cough, or breathe, do nothing.

1. Stand behind the person.
2. Make a fist with one hand and place it above her belly button, just below the rib cage.
3. Grasp the fist with the other hand.
4. Push your fist in and up quickly.
5. Keep doing this until the person can spit out the object and breathe and speak.

If this doesn't work, call the doctor, hospital, or local emergency assistance number.

Fractures, Sprains, Broken Bones

Do not move the injured person. Keep the person calm. Call the emergency number.

Frostbite

Frostbite occurs when part of the body starts to freeze. The skin turns white, grayish-yellow, or pale blue. As quickly as possible, warm the area. Put the frozen area into warm (not hot) water. Dry very gently (do not rub or press hard) and wrap in warm clothing, blankets, or both. Call a doctor, hospital, or local emergency assistance number.

Hyperthermia

This is what happens when a person gets too much body heat. If it is a mild case, it's called heat exhaustion; a severe case is heat stroke. Get the person out of the sun and cool her off. Have her slowly drink cool (not cold) water. Call a doctor if the person is very hot, not sweating, pale, nauseous, has trouble breathing, and seems dazed.

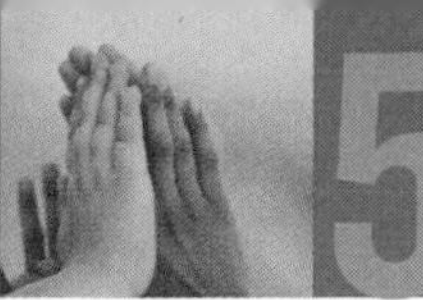

Hypothermia
This is what happens when someone has too little body heat. Get the person out of the cold and warm her body slowly. Remove wet clothing and cover with dry clothing or blankets. If the person is conscious (awake) and able to swallow, give warm liquids. Call a doctor, hospital, or local emergency assistance number.

Insect Stings
Remove the stinger if you can. Don't use tweezers, because this might cause poison to travel into the bitten area. Instead, scrape across the top of the skin. Wash the area with soap and water, and apply ice to reduce the swelling. If there is a lot of swelling, or if the person seems to be getting sick, she might be suffering an allergic reaction. In this case, call a doctor, hospital, or local emergency assistance number.

Nosebleed
Have the person sit forward with her head bent slightly forward. Pinch the lower part of her nose for at least five minutes to stop the bleeding. Then place a cold, wet cloth on her nose and face.

Poisoning
Call your local poison control center or a doctor for help immediately.

Shock
This can occur in any kind of emergency. The symptoms are sweating, rapid breathing, nausea, and cold or clammy skin. Keep the person lying down. Raise the feet. Place one cloth or blanket under the person and another cloth or blanket over her. Try to keep her comfortable and calm. Call a doctor, hospital, or local emergency assistance number.

Snakebite
If you don't know whether the snake was poisonous, treat it as poisonous. First, calm the person. (Keeping a person calm makes her blood, and the poison, move more slowly.) Get her to a doctor or hospital as soon as possible. If you can, carry her so the poison doesn't circulate too quickly.

Splinter
Gently wash the area with soap and water. Look for the edge of the splinter and try to pull it out using your clean fingertips or tweezers. Be careful not to push the splinter under the skin.

Sunburn
Gently soak the burned area in cold water. Do not put ice on the area. If the person is in a great deal of pain, call a doctor.

Tick Bite
Put tweezers as close to the tick's head as possible and pull the tick out. Save the tick so a doctor can test it for Lyme and other diseases. (Tape it onto a piece of white paper.)

Home Safety

It's important to keep your home safe. Prevention is the key. Many things in a home, when not used properly, can be dangerous. Learn how to *prevent* accidents—such as poisoning or fires—from happening.

Put Poisons in Their Place

To prevent poisoning, look through your home for things that might be poisonous, such as medicines and cleaning fluids. Even certain plants, when eaten, can be poisonous!

With the help of an adult, store all poisons in a safe place—out of reach of young children. Be sure that all bottles are labeled, especially if a poisonous fluid has been poured into a different container than the one it came in.

Fire Safety

There are two very important parts to good fire safety.

1. Learn how to prevent fires from starting. (See the illustration to the right for the most common mistakes people make in their home.)
2. Know what to do should you find yourself in a fire. (See the next section.)

Look at these illustrations. They demonstrate STOP—DROP—ROLL, which is the technique to use if your clothes or another person's clothes catch on fire.

1. **STOP** where you are (or get the person to STOP).

2. **DROP** to the floor or ground. (Or get the person to DROP.) Do not run.

3. **ROLL** back and forth, making sure to cover your face with your hands. Or wrap a coat, blanket, or rug around you (or the other person) to smother the flames.

Activity:

Fire Hazard Hidden Picture

How many fire hazards can you find in this house? Circle them! When you have finished, turn to the end of this chapter to see a list of the fire hazards in the picture. How many did you spot? Go back and find the ones you missed.

Fire Safety Rules

If fire does break out at home, remember these rules:

1. Get yourself and other people out of the house quickly.
2. Do not go back for anything or anyone.
3. Do not try to put the fire out. Fires spread very quickly.
4. Call the fire department from outside the house. Give your name and address and the exact place of the fire. If you use a fire alarm box, stay near it so you can direct the fire truck once it arrives.

If smoke comes into a room and the door is closed:

1. Do not open the door.
2. Feel the door. If it is cool, open it a little and hold it with your foot.
3. Feel the air outside with your hand. If the air is not hot, make your way out of the building immediately.
4. Use stairs or fire escapes. Do NOT use elevators.
5. If the door is warm, block the crack under the door with pillows, sheets, blankets, or a rug. Go to the window and yell for help. Stay near the window until help arrives.
6. Cover your nose and mouth with a wet cloth, if possible, and wet the materials you are using to block the door.

If you wake up and the room is full of smoke:

1. Roll out of the bed directly onto the floor.
2. Crawl to the nearest exit. Smoke rises, so the coolest, freshest air will be close to the floor.
3. Remember: Do not open any door without first checking to see if it is warm!

If fire breaks out in a public place:

When you are in a public place, such as a department store or movie theater, always take a minute to look around to find where the fire exits, or quickest ways out are. If fire breaks out when you are in a public place:

1. Stay calm.
2. Walk quickly and quietly to the nearest exit.

Do More

If this topic interests you, check out the "Safety First" badge in the *Junior Girl Scout Badge Book.*

Safety First

Activity:

Fire Safety

Here are three activities you and your troop can do:

1

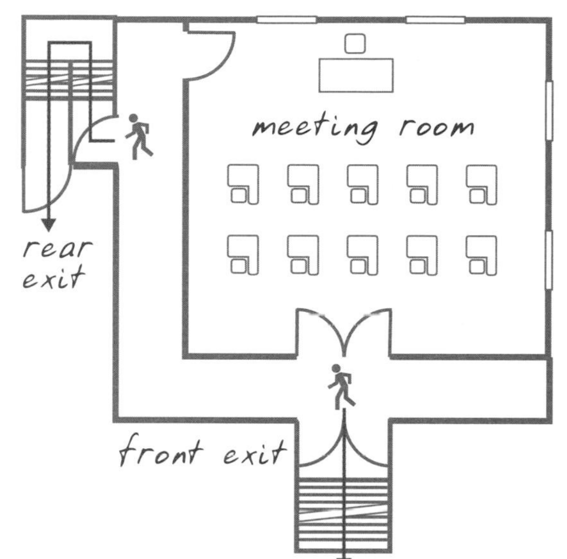

Plan and practice fire escape routes. Draw a fire escape plan for the place where your troop or group meets. Be sure to include at least two ways to escape.

2

Invite a firefighter to visit and speak to your troop or group to go over fire safety and prevention.

3

Find out how a smoke detector works and where to place one in an apartment, house, troop meeting place, or other location.

Protect Yourself

Most people are good and kind. But unfortunately, people you know, as well as people you don't know, can hurt you. Learn how to protect yourself from abuse—treatment that hurts you or is harmful—and how to tell someone you trust if you have been abused.

If you have been abused, tell someone. You might feel ashamed or embarrassed. You might even think the abuse was your fault. But it wasn't! No one should hurt you, no matter what you say or do. If you are afraid to tell a grown-up you know, most communities have hotlines, or you can call the police. If you know someone who is being abused, convince her to tell a grown-up.

You can learn to protect yourself by avoiding situations that might be dangerous. However, if someone does harm you, try to remember:

- What happened?
- When did it happen?
- Where did it happen?
- Who was there?
- What did the person (or persons) look like?

Activity:

Memory Game

If someone you don't know harms you, it's important to try to remember as much as you can about the person. Also, if you see someone hurting someone else, you can help by remembering things like: What did the person's car look like? What was the person wearing? What was the person's height, hair, or eye color? (You can compare them to an adult you know.)

Let's see how good your memory is. Look at this picture for 30 seconds, then cover it up. See how many of the questions below you can answer. No peeking!

1. What color is the woman's hair?

2. Is she wearing glasses?

3. What kind of dog is she walking?

4. What is the woman carrying?

5. What kind of car is in the picture?

6. What is the license plate of the car?

7. What are the street names?

8. Name at least one of the stores in the picture.

Protect Yourself

Personal Safety Do's and Don'ts

When You Are Out

do

Scream or yell for help if someone tries to get you to go with him or her. You can yell "Fire!" or "Help! This person is not my parent" or "Help! I don't know this person."

Go to a police station, store sales person, or a uniformed official if you feel you are being followed or if something is making you nervous.

don't

Play in deserted areas or out-of-the-way places, like alleys, dead-end streets, construction sites, empty laundry rooms, abandoned buildings, rooftops and elevators, train tracks, truck yards, quarries, or vacant lots.

Believe a message a stranger gives you like, "Your mother wants me to bring you home."

When You're Home Alone

do

Keep all doors and windows locked.

Know how to answer the phone when you are home alone. Don't tell a stranger who has called that you are home alone. If someone asks for a grown-up, simply say they can't come to the phone right now and take a message. Practice answering the phone with members of your Girl Scout troop or group or with family members.

Call the police or your emergency assistance number if you hear or see someone trying to break into your home.

don't

Open the door to a stranger, even if he or she is in uniform and has a package or flowers to deliver. Tell the person to come back another time, or have them leave the package outside. Whatever you do, don't open the door.

Give a person who calls the "wrong" number your telephone number, even if he or she insists. Just say, "You have the wrong number."

Test Yourself: *Personal Safety Role-Playing*

What would you do in these situations?

1. You wake up in the night when someone you know is sitting on your bed and touching you in places that make you feel uncomfortable.

2. One of the older boys in the neighborhood asks if you want to play "special grown-up games" with him. He says you have to promise not to tell.

3. You are at the shopping mall with your grandmother when you see this great pair of shoes in a store window. You run over to look. When you turn around, you can't see your grandmother.

4. You are at the movies with friends. A man sits next to you and accidentally brushes your leg and says, "Sorry." When the movie starts, he does it again.

Possible Solutions

1. You could ask the person to leave, yell for an adult to come, get up and go find an adult.
2. Tell him no and walk away, then tell an adult you trust.
3. Go to the cashier in a store and ask her to get the mall security.
4. Get up and tell the movie theater manager.

MORE SAFETY ACTIVITIES

Read the decision-making story maze later in this chapter. A lot of the choices involve staying safe. Create your own safety story or safety skit that has different endings depending upon the path you choose.

Find out about bicycle safety. Learn how to inspect and safely ride a bicycle. Find out about riding in-line skates, skateboards, or scooters safely. What kind of body protection do you need for each of these sports?

Plan a safety awareness event for National Safe Kids Week (the first week in May each year). Maybe you and your Girl Scout troop or group could act out some of the safety lessons from this chapter, such as STOP-DROP-ROLL or what to do when a stranger knocks on your door.

Pick a sport and create a safety checklist, poster, or booklet for that sport. See the "Be Healthy, Be Fit" chapter for sports ideas.

Crazy About Computers

More Girl Scouts than ever before know how to use computers and are involved in activities like:

- Earning a Girl Scout badge about technology
- Communicating by e-mail
- Finding and using information from the Internet
- Creating personal Web sites

In fact, as you might already know, GSUSA maintains a Web site, "Just for Girls," that provides information about Girl Scouting. Girls from all over the country and from other parts of the world send their ideas to the "Just for Girls" section of the Girl Scout Web site *www.girlscouts.org/girls*

Being Safe Online

The Internet is an amazing place. You can get help for your homework, do research for a paper, or chat with a person from the other side of the world.

There's only one problem: You can't tell who you are really chatting with in a computer chat room. Chat rooms might be a lot of fun to visit, but you also need to know some safety rules. And while the Internet might be an incredible place to wander through, you can find information on it that is not appropriate for young people to see or read.

Did You Know?

You need to get permission from the author or publisher of videos and music if you are going to put them on a Web site or want to post words to copyrighted songs.

Cyberspace Safety

Read the online safety pledge below. Discuss the cyberspace safety rules in the pledge with your parent, guardian, or Girl Scout leader. Afterwards, sign the pledge.

My Online Safety Pledge

I **will not** give out personal information such as my address, telephone number, parents' or guardian's work address/telephone number, or the name and location of my school without the permission of my parents or guardian.

I **will tell** an adult right away if I come across any information that makes me feel uncomfortable.

I **will never agree** to get together with someone I "meet" online without first checking with my parents or guardian. If my parents or guardian agree to the meeting, I will arrange it in a public place and bring a parent or guardian along.

I **will never send** a person my picture or anything else without first checking with my parents or guardian.

I **will not respond** to any messages that are mean or that in any way make me uncomfortable. It is not my fault if I get a message like that. If I do, I will tell my parents or guardian right away so that they can contact the online service.

I **will talk** with my parents or guardian so that we can set up rules for going online. We will decide on the time of day that I can be online, the length of time I can be online, and appropriate areas for me to visit. I will not access other areas or break these rules without their permission.

Girl Scout ____________________ **Date** __________

Parent, Guardian, or Adult Partner ____________________ **Date** __________

Making Decisions

You make decisions every day. Some are easy: choosing your clothes for school, figuring out what to eat for breakfast, picking out a new book to read. Some are not so easy: choosing between sitting with one group of friends or another at lunch, deciding between the soccer team or the swim team for an after-school activity, or figuring out how to tell your parents about a test on which you did badly.

Sometimes you have so many different choices that decision-making can be hard and confusing. People might also try to convince you to make a choice you really don't want to make. Making tough decisions is just that—tough!

Taking Risks

Sometimes it's okay to make a decision even though you don't know exactly what the result will be. You might, for example, decide to join the math team in order to improve your skills or to try out for the school play even though you are shy. Those are healthy risks. On the other hand, if you decide to try a cigarette just because all your friends are doing it, you are taking an unhealthy risk.

Each decision you make will have consequences. Some consequences are good: You might realize you are really talented at math once you are on the team. Some consequences aren't so good: Smoking cigarettes can not only get you into trouble with your parents, but can also damage your health.

Real-Life Decisions

Ask someone you know to tell you about a difficult decision she had to make. Maybe your mom decided to go back to school to prepare for a new career. Maybe your aunt decided to go out for the football team even though some of her friends made fun of her.

Ask her if she would make the same choice now. What were the good points and bad points (pros and cons) of the choice she made? Did she ask for help when making her decision?

Think about a tough decision you recently had to make. If you had different choices, did you look at the good points and bad points of each choice? Did you talk to people about your choices? Are you happy with the decision you made?

HOW TO Make a Decision

When making a tough decision, it sometimes helps to follow a step-by-step process. Using the steps below might help you determine the best choice. You might not need every step, except when making big decisions.

1. **Figure out the problem or issue.**
2. **Collect information about yourself and the situation; think about your values, goals, and interests.**
3. **Think of as many solutions to the problem as you possibly can.**
4. **Look at the good points and bad points (pros and cons) of each solution.**
5. **Make a decision.**
6. **Take action.**
7. **Evaluate: Are you happy with the decision you made?**

Think about a tough decision you recently made. How might these steps have helped you? Try using these steps to help with your next decision.

A Decision-Making Story Maze

Have some fun with the following story maze. It will show just how much one decision can affect another, just like a row of dominos toppling over. In this story maze, you get to be the main character. Follow the story wherever it leads you. Notice what choices you make and what the consequences are.

You and your best friend Monique are on your way home from school. Up ahead, you see the new girl in your class, Tina. You and Monique catch up with her. Tina invites you and Monique to her house. Monique decides to go. You know that you are supposed to go straight to your neighbor's house from school. What do you do? If you say, "I can't, I have to go home right after school," go to A. If you say, "Sure, but only for a little while," go to C.

A

You cross the street and continue on your way. When you reach your neighbor's home, no one is there. You think this is strange. Something must have happened for her to not be there.

- If you go into the backyard to do your homework and wait, go to B.
- If you try to catch up with Tina and Monique, go to I.

I

You run to the corner where you left Monique and Tina. You don't see them. You don't know where Tina lives, so you head back to your neighbor's house. You decide to take a shortcut through the park. You see a group of older kids who are smoking. You recognize one of them. She calls you over and introduces you to her friends. They ask if you would like a cigarette.

- If you say "No thanks!" and walk away, go to J.
- If you take one, go to H.

H

You decide that you won't smoke it, but you will just stand there holding it when you hear a car horn. You slowly turn to look and it's your neighbor with a very upset look on her face. You throw down the cigarette and run to the car. You keep saying that you weren't really smoking, but you know that your parents are going to be really mad when they find out. **THE END.**

G

Your father tells you he'll be right there. On the way home, he tells you that you should have known better than to get in a car with strangers or people you don't know well. He continues to talk about all of the things that could have happened to you, and now you will be grounded for a month. **THE END.**

You've just finished your math assignment when your neighbor comes into the backyard. "I'm so glad you waited for me," she says. "I was stuck in the worst traffic jam." **THE END.**

C

When you get to Tina's house, her teenage brother and his two friends are the only ones there. You know your parents don't want you visiting a friend when there are no adults present. You tell Monique you think you should leave. Just then Tina's brother offers to take everyone to the mall. Everyone thinks it's a good idea.

- If you go to the mall, go to D.
- If you say "Good-bye" and go on to your neighbor's home, go to E.

You hear the older kids calling after you saying things like "wimp," "baby," and "nerd," but you don't care. You know that you want to stay healthy. **THE END.**

D

You all pile into Tina's brother's car and go to the mall. The teenagers decide to go off by themselves and say they'll meet you in an hour. Tina, Monique, and you go into a music store. Tina and Monique go down one aisle. You go down another. The next thing you know, Tina and Monique are gone. You think that maybe they are hiding. You look all over the store. You can't find them. The cashier says she thinks she saw them leave.

- If you call your father who works nearby to pick you up, go to G.
- If you go to the information booth and have them paged, go to F.

Tina's brother and his friends meet you at the information booth. So do Tina and Monique. They apologize for playing a trick on you and decide to leave the mall. They drop you off at your neighbor's home. When you get there, she is very upset with you for being late. She says she'll have to tell your parents when they get home. **THE END.**

When you reach your neighbor's house, she says that she expected you home sooner, and was just about to call the school. You apologize and start doing your homework. **THE END.**

Cigarettes, Drugs, & Alcohol Aren't Coo

Avoiding harmful substances like tobacco, alcohol, and marijuana is an important part of personal safety. You risk your good health and shorten your life if you put harmful substances into your body.

Why You Should Say "No"

- Harmful substances can have an extra bad effect on your growing body.
- They can affect the way you play sports or do other activities, making it harder to play well.
- Harmful substances can lead to cancer, stroke, heart disease, emphysema (a deadly disease that makes it very hard to breathe), and many other serious illnesses.
- You can become addicted. That means you would not be able to stop using the substances, even if you wanted to. (Did you know that most adults who smoke became addicted by the time they were 13 years old?)
- Women who smoke, drink, or use drugs while pregnant can hurt their unborn babies.
- If you start using harmful substances, you might stop doing the things that once were important to you: homework, sports, or being with friends.
- Harmful substances can affect the way you look, smell, and act. For example, smoking makes your hair, breath, and clothing smell bad.
- Harmful substances cost a lot of money. You might end up with no money for the things you enjoy—movies, magazines, clothes—because of how much you are spending on the addictive substance.
- Becoming addicted will conflict with your moral and personal values.
- Cigarette smoke contains thousands of chemicals. Over 40 of them cause cancer: arsenic, butane, carbon dioxide, nicotine, and tar are among them. Girl Scouts has an anti-smoking activity booklet, *Girl Scouts Against Smoking.* You can receive a patch after you have finished some of the activities from this booklet. The activities in this section can also help you earn the anti-smoking patch. The booklet and patch are available through your Girl Scout council.

How Cool Can It Be?

You might find that friends use harmful drugs and encourage you to join them. No matter what the reason for using drugs—to look more "grown up," to be a part of the group, to stop feeling bored—it's a mistake. You should say NO to harmful drugs, cigarettes, and alcohol.

Secondhand Smoke

Smoke from other people's cigarettes is called secondhand smoke. When you breathe in the smoke of people smoking near you, you can harm your health, too. Breathing in secondhand smoke can cause these problems:

- Coughing
- Wheezing
- Itchy eyes
- Runny nose
- Sore throat
- Headaches
- Colds
- Ear infections
- Asthma
- Heart attack
- Cancer

WORD SEARCH

Here are some words that have to do with smoking and second-hand smoke. Circle each word you find. The hidden words can go across, up, down, or diagonally. Check the next page for the answers.

ADDICTED
CANCER
COUGHING
LUNG
NICOTINE
SMELL
SMOKE
TAR
TASTE
TOBACCO

T	C	A	N	C	E	R	E	G
S	O	R	B	A	H	K	J	N
R	A	B	T	N	O	Y	L	I
A	N	B	A	M	R	D	L	H
T	E	F	S	C	I	D	U	G
E	N	I	T	O	C	I	N	U
K	L	L	E	M	S	O	G	O
A	D	D	I	C	T	E	D	C

Alcohol Alert

The alcohol in beer, wine, wine coolers, and liquor is very powerful. You can overdose and die from drinking too much alcohol! Or you can lose your good judgment and do something you'll be sorry about later. Some people who think they know exactly when to stop drinking fool themselves because alcohol is very sneaky. The part of the brain that would say "that's enough" or "time to stop" gets turned off by the alcohol. So you can easily drink too much and do some very foolish things.

WORD SEARCH
ANSWERS

T	C	A	N	C	E	R	E	G
S	O	R	B	A	H	K	J	N
R	A	B	T	N	O	Y	L	I
A	N	B	A	M	R	D	L	H
T	E	F	S	C	I	D	U	G
E	N	I	T	O	C	I	N	U
K	L	L	E	M	S	O	G	O
A	D	D	I	C	T	E	D	C

Ways to Avoid Alcohol

So why take that first drink of alcohol? A lot of kids take their first drink because friends pressure them. It is very hard not to drink or smoke if your friends do. But if people are trying so hard to get you to do something that is dangerous or something that you don't want to do, maybe they are not really your friends. Read about how to deal with peer pressure in the "Family and Friends" chapter. You can find suggestions about how to say NO in the *Girl Scouts Against Smoking* booklet.

Find Healthy—Not Harmful—Activities

Think of activities that you can do alone or with friends rather than just "hang out." Sometimes, you have to take a healthy risk and be the leader of your group by taking up a sport, hobby, or some other activity that would be a lot healthier than taking drugs. Get ideas for different activities from the "Create and Invent" and "Be Healthy, Be Fit" chapters. Find three activities that look interesting, try them, and introduce them to your friends.

Adults Can Drink—Why Can't I?

Perhaps you've seen adults drink alcohol from time to time. It's important to remember that many adults make responsible choices for themselves—which might include drinking in a safe and reasonable way. Children and teens are not ready to make those types of choices.

Do More

If this section was of interest to you, check out the "High on Life" and "A Healthier You" badges in your *Junior Girl Scout Badge Book.*

High on Life

A Healthier You

Fire Hazard Hidden Picture: Answer Key

6 Be Healthy, Be Fit

In This Chapter You Will Learn About:

"To make yourself strong and healthy, it is necessary to begin with your inside. Get the blood into good order and the heart to work well."

— JULIETTE GORDON LOW

Think of all the things you want to do in one day! You need a healthy body and lots of energy. Being able to take care of yourself—whether it's by preparing a healthy lunch or organizing an exercise group—can make you feel good, inside and out.

This chapter is all about exercise and eating right, which will help you keep your body strong, healthy, and ready for anything!

Aerobic Exercise

You probably already do a lot of aerobic exercise. Just think of things you do that make you get a bit out of breath: dancing, skating, jumping rope, bicycling, walking, running, and swimming. These are all aerobic activities because they consist of continuous movements that keep the heart beating faster.

Your heart is a muscle. By making the heart beat faster, you make it stronger. As your heart grows stronger, it takes less effort to do the same amount of physical work.

Note: Before you start an exercise program you should get a check-up from your doctor.

Activity:

Start Exercising

Do an aerobic activity at least three times a week, for at least 20 to 30 minutes. There are some activities you can do alone or with a friend (walking, biking, skating), and some you can do as part of a team (soccer, basketball). Switch activities so you won't be bored. It does not matter what you do—as long as you get your heart pumping faster for at least 20 minutes.

Some sports are more aerobic than others. Swimming, basketball, soccer, and skating are good aerobic sports.

Keep an exercise journal to see how much progress you make. Write down the date and time of exercise, the type of exercise, if you exercised with a partner, and how you felt while you were exercising that day.

Games Can Be Exercise, Too

These games might seem like play to you, but they are also great exercise. Give them a try!

Activity:

El Reloj A Jump Rope Game from Argentina

During the summer in Argentina, young people play a popular game that is also a great aerobic exercise. It is called *El Reloj* (pronounced *el re-LOH*). It means "the clock." You can enjoy *El Reloj,* too.

What You Need

- Four to 12 players
- A long jump rope

What You Do

1. Two players hold each end of the rope and swing it. The other players stand in line.
2. The first player jumps over the rope once and says, "One o'clock."
3. The second player jumps over the rope twice and says, "Two o'clock."
4. The game continues until a player reaches twelve o'clock and jumps rope 12 times without missing. If a player misses, everyone must start at the beginning.

Bonus. Call out the hours in Spanish, the way they do in Argentina.

English	*Spanish*	*Pronunciation*
One o'clock	*Es la una*	*ehs la oo-na*
Two o'clock	*Son las dos*	*sone lahs doce*
Three o'clock	*Son las tres*	*sone lahs tress*
Four o'clock	*Son las cuatro*	*sone lahs KWA-tro*
Five o'clock	*Son las cinco*	*sone lahs SIN-ko*
Six o'clock	*Son las seis*	*sone lahs sace*
Seven o'clock	*Son las siete*	*sone lahs see-EH-teh*
Eight o'clock	*Son las ocho*	*sone lahs O-cho*
Nine o'clock	*Son las nueve*	*sone lahs noo-EH-veh*
Ten o'clock	*Son las diez*	*sone lahs DEE-es*
Eleven o'clock	*Son las once*	*sone lahs OHN-seh*
Twelve o'clock	*Son las doce*	*sone lahs DOE-seh*

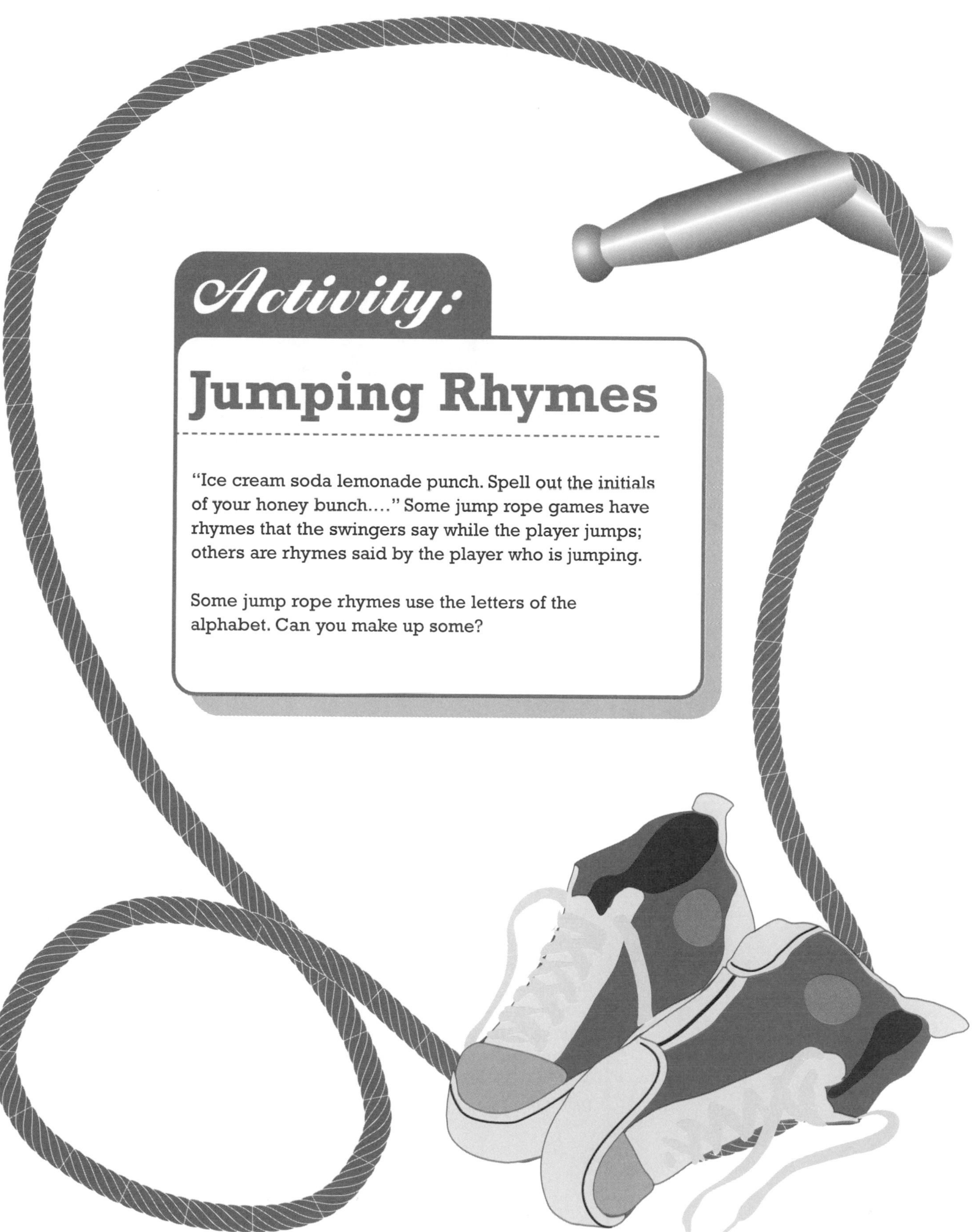

Activity:

Jumping Rhymes

"Ice cream soda lemonade punch. Spell out the initials of your honey bunch...." Some jump rope games have rhymes that the swingers say while the player jumps; others are rhymes said by the player who is jumping.

Some jump rope rhymes use the letters of the alphabet. Can you make up some?

Games Can Be Exercise, Too

Activity: Relay Racing

Make up your own relay race. Decide how many parts there will be. Here's one idea. What others can you think of?

- The first person runs without moving her arms.
- The second person runs balancing a book on her head.
- The third person runs or walks backwards.
- The fourth person hops on one foot.
- The fifth person runs as fast as she can.

Can you think of some props and obstacles that would make your relay race even more challenging and fun?

You can create your own rules to other games, such as hula hoop, handball, kick-the-can, tag. Try it!

Activity: Indonesia's *Main Karet Gelang*

Main karet gelang (main ka-RET ge-LANG) means "rubber band game." Young people in Indonesia make a wad, or ball, of rubber bands and take turns kicking it into the air. The object is to kick the wad as long as possible without it hitting the ground.

What You Need

About 30 rubber bands (use different colors to make the ball look cool). Tie two together in the middle and keep wrapping bands around each other to make a ball. You can use a small rubber ball, though the game won't be exactly like the one that Indonesians play.

What You Do

Two to ten or more players divide into teams.

1. One player from a team tosses the rubber-band ball into the air and kicks it with one foot.
2. That player or any of the others keep kicking it so it doesn't touch the ground.
3. Count your kicks, or have someone on the opposite team count them.
4. Once the ball hits the ground, the other team gets a turn.
5. The player or team who keeps the ball in the air for the most kicks wins.
6. Keep taking turns, seeing how many kicks you can get!

Activity:

Hopscotch Like Girls in the Netherlands

There are so many kinds of hopscotch games that girls all over the world play. You can make up your own or try this one from the Netherlands: *Zondag* to *Zaterdag* (Sunday to Saturday) Dutch children draw eight squares. The first four squares, and the last two, are in a straight line. The fifth and sixth squares are next to each other. (See illustration.) The first square is left blank inside. The days of the week are written in the others, starting with Monday.

What You Need

- Chalk
- Two or more players

Rules:

1. Players lose a turn if they step on lines, stumble, land on two feet, or toss the pebble into the wrong box.
2. When a player loses a turn, she has to leave her pebble on the square until her next turn. Other players must hop over it; they can't land in her square.

What You Do

1. Stand on the blank square and toss a pebble that must land inside the Monday square.
2. Hop on one leg from the Sunday square to Tuesday, but DO NOT land on the Monday square. As you hop, you must say the day of the week you are hopping to.
3. Hop on the same leg to the Wednesday square, and then to each day of the week.
4. When you get back to Sunday, you can stand on both feet. Hop backwards through the week to the blank square again.
5. Next, toss your pebble onto Tuesday. Hop from Monday to Wednesday without landing on the Tuesday square.
6. Repeat the process through the days of the week.
7. After the first player has completed going through the days of the week, it is the next player's turn. See the rules for what happens if a player makes a mistake.

Days of the week in Dutch:

English	*Dutch*	*Pronunciation*
Sunday	*Zondag*	*ZONE-dahg*
Monday	*Maandag*	*MAHN-dahg*
Tuesday	*Dinsdag*	*DINS-dahg*
Wednesday	*Woensdag*	*WOE-ens-dahg*
Thursday	*Donderdag*	*DON-der-dahg*
Friday	*Vrijdag*	*VRAY-dahg*
Saturday	*Zaterdag*	*ZAH-ter-dahg*

Play Sports!

Which sport is right for you? With so many different sports and fitness activities to choose from, how do you decide? You can try them all or narrow your search by answering a few questions. Use the list of sports here for help.

Archery

Badminton

Basketball

Biking

Canoeing

Cheerleading

Cross-Country Skiing

Dance

Downhill Skiing

Field Hockey

Golf

Gymnastics

Hiking

Ice Hockey

Ice Skating

In-line Skating

Kayaking

Mountain Biking

Racquetball

Rock Climbing

Skateboarding

Soccer

Softball

Squash

Swimming

Tennis

Track and Field

Volleyball

Test Yourself: *Find the Sports for You*

1. Where can you play sports in your community? Find out what sports the local Parks and Recreation Department and your school have to offer, such as basketball, soccer, gymnastics, cheerleading, softball, volleyball, swimming, and track and field.
2. Do you prefer to exercise indoors or outdoors? Do you prefer to exercise alone, with a friend, or with a group of friends? If these preferences make a difference to your enjoyment, pick your sport carefully.
3. When it comes to sports, do you like to take risks?
   A. *Yes.* Try sports like ice skating, skateboarding, cheerleading, gymnastics, and rock climbing.
   B. *Sometimes.* Try field events (pole vault, high jump), basketball, or volleyball.
   C. *No.* Try sports like golf, track, or archery.

Following Up

Based on your answers:

1. Pick a sport or two that you would like to try or learn more about.
2. Get information about the sport from your school gym teacher or coach, or from the Internet.
3. Watch a game on TV, rent a video, or watch a competition in person in order to learn more about the sport. Some good places to watch competitions are at high schools, colleges or universities, or at professional sporting events. You can become an expert—even if you don't play!
4. Learn the rules of the sport, the equipment needed, and the amount of time required for practice.
5. Find out where in your community these sports are offered and how much the ones you would like to try cost (rental of tennis court, ice skating lessons, dance lessons).

Getting Started with a Sport

You have found a sport you want to try—GREAT! Once you have signed up for a sport, here's a short checklist of things to do before your first practice.

- ☐ Buy, rent, or borrow the equipment you will need. Make sure it is in good condition and that it fits!
- ☐ Get into shape. Do the "Fun and Fit" badge from your *Junior Girl Scout Badge Book* to get into tip-top condition.
- ☐ Eat right and get plenty of rest. Do the "Highway to Health" badge to learn more about your body and how to eat right.
- ☐ Get ready to learn something new and meet new friends!

Stay Positive!

The first time you try a new sport, you might feel frustrated. Don't worry! Learning something new takes a lot of time. Be patient and kind to yourself and hang in there. You *will* get better with practice.

Sports Diary

Once you have started playing a sport, keep a sports diary. A sports diary is a place for you to write down your goals for your sport, a place to write down what you did well and what you would like to improve upon. You can also keep track of how often you practice and how you felt during practice. Design your own diary or use the *Sports Diary for Junior Girl Scouts.*

Sports Tips

1. Before you start, get your body ready to go. Always stretch your muscles before you get started. This can reduce your chance of injury. Warm up your body by doing jumping jacks or by taking a short jog.
2. After you practice or play, do a cool-down (perhaps another short jog) to let your body relax.
3. After the cool-down, stretch to keep your muscles flexible.
4. Use equipment that is in good condition.
5. Practice or play in an area that is safe and free of hazards.
6. Drink water before, during, and after you play, especially when it is hot!
7. Stop playing if you get hurt or feel tired.

Be a Good Sport

Sports are about much more than just exercise. Another important part of playing sports is learning to be a good sport. Here's how:

- Have fun.
- Encourage yourself and others.
- Play by the rules.
- Treat others as you would like to be treated.
- Respect and stick to decisions made by coaches and officials.
- Give your best effort.
- Control your temper.
- Live the Girl Scout Law.

Do More

There are many sports-related badge activities in the *Junior Girl Scout Badge Book,* such as:

Adventure Sports

Court Sports

Field Sports

Sports Sampler

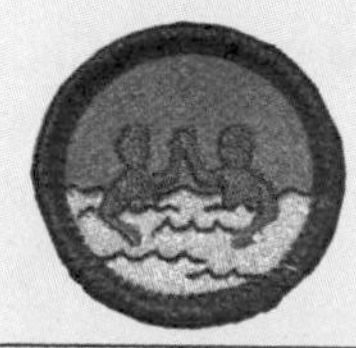

Swimming

Winter Sports

Eating Right

"An apple a day keeps the doctor away!"

"You must eat three square meals a day!"

"Eat all your vegetables!"

Your parents probably grew up hearing at least one of these phrases. Maybe they used a couple of them on you. You already know you should eat healthy foods. But sometimes it can be tough to eat things you don't like.

Nutrition News

Good news for snack lovers! You can get all the nutrition you need each day by eating five or six little meals, instead of three large ones. And thanks to the U.S. Department of Agriculture, you have the Food Guide Pyramid, which shows the foods you should eat daily, and how much of each you need.

No Dull Diets!

The key to good nutrition is to eat a variety of foods. That means it is okay to have a few sweets, as long as most of your food intake is healthy. What the food pyramid shows is that you should eat more of the foods from the bottom of the pyramid and less of the foods on the top, which means you will be eating many vegetables, fruits, and foods that are high in complex carbohydrates and fiber.

That doesn't call for a dull diet. That calls for a varied diet. If you seem to eat the same five or six foods again and again, it's time to find ways to add new foods to your daily diet. Your taste buds will thank you for it!

Pasta

Fish

Do More

If nutrition interests you, check out "Food Power" or "Let's Get Cooking" in the *Junior Girl Scout Badge Book.*

Food Power

Let's Get Cooking

Swiss Chard

Sushi

Eggs

Pear

Tomatoes

Test Yourself: *Where Do Your Foods Fit In?*

You can learn a lot about food groups by looking at the pyramid. Which foods should you eat most often? Less often? Keep a food diary for a few days—write down everything you eat—then ask yourself:

1. Where do the foods I eat fit on the Food Guide Pyramid?
2. What foods should I be eating more of?
3. What foods should I be eating less of?
4. Talk to your parent or guardian about making changes in the foods you eat so you are eating better.

Eat a Variety of Foods

The more varied your diet is, the more likely you will get all of the nutrients (vitamins and minerals) you need. Topping the list of nutrients that girls and women need are iron, calcium, fiber, and protein. See if you can build a diet of different foods that contain these nutrients. Circle at least one of the foods you will try from each of these categories.

Iron
Needed for red blood cells (which carry oxygen). A lack of iron can lead to shortness of breath, anemia (a disease where you have less than the normal number of red blood cells), and delayed physical development. Unless you are vegetarian, you probably get most of your iron from meat.

Try adding: instant oatmeal, canned apricots (in water), or sunflower seeds to your weekly diet.

Calcium
Needed for strong bones and teeth. You probably get most of your calcium from milk or dairy products, such as cheese, yogurt, and ice cream.

Try adding: calcium-fortified orange juice, Parmesan cheese, cooked spinach or collard greens.

Fiber
Reduces the risk of heart disease, helps you control your weight by making you feel fuller, and keeps food moving through your digestive system. You get fiber whenever you eat a sandwich. Bread is a good source of fiber, especially if it is whole wheat bread.

Try adding: baked beans, broccoli, pears, apples, oranges (most fruits are full of fiber), carrots, dry-roasted peanuts.

Protein
Builds and repairs your muscles. Lean (not fatty) meat is a common source of protein.

Try adding: white tuna, scrambled eggs, bean and rice burrito, a smoothie with nonfat milk, tofu.

Which foods did you select from each category?

Iron: ______________________________

____

Calcium: ______________________________

____

Fiber: ______________________________

____

Protein: ______________________________

____

Plan a weekly menu. Vary your diet with your new foods. Use the Food Guide Pyramid to help you.

Snack Smart

Need a midday, late-night, how-am-I-ever-going-to-finish-my-homework munchie?

Grab one of these healthy snacks:

Fresh fruit

Low-fat granola bar

Popcorn (see recipes in the "Family and Friends" chapter)

Nuts

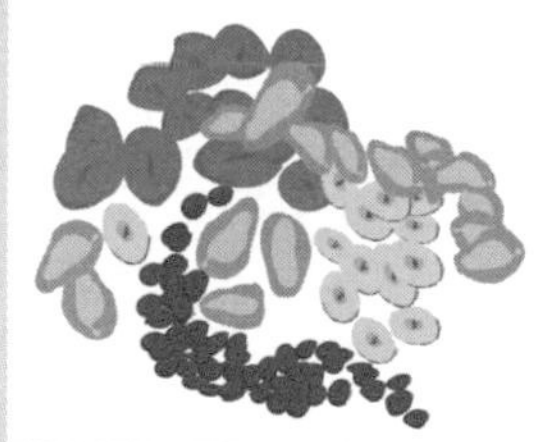

Dried fruit

Pre-cut celery and carrot sticks

Peanut butter and crackers
Low-fat cheese and crackers

Pretzels

Hard-boiled eggs

Create a troop or group recipe for a delicious, nutritious snack food. Prepare your snack for meetings or trips.

A Year's Worth of Healthy Eating

When is the best time to develop healthy eating habits? *Right now!* Begin with the current season of the year, and work your way through each season with fun recipes and good times.

Autumn

It's apple-picking time! Plan a field trip to the countryside orchards. But what are you to do with all the apples when you return?

Why not make: applesauce, apple pie, apple butter, applesauce cake, cinnamon baked apples, apple oatmeal cookies, apple and noodles, Norwegian baked apples (with shredded cheese, pecans, and raisins), or curried apples and shrimp? Or cut them up in salads. Of course, you can just eat them plain! (You can find lots of recipes on Internet Web sites. Search for "apple recipes.")

Activity:

Apple Crisp

Ingredients:

- 6 apples, peeled and sliced (have an adult supervise)
- 3/4 cup* flour
- 3/4 cup* oats
- 1 cup* brown sugar
- 1 teaspoon* cinnamon
- 1 teaspoon* nutmeg
- 1 stick butter, softened
- 1/4 cup* apple juice or water

Directions:

1. Place half the peeled apples in a greased 9x9-inch* pan.
2. Mix the dry ingredients and butter together.
3. Crumble half over the apples.
4. Add the remaining apples.
5. Cover with the rest of the dry mixture.
6. Pour juice over top.
7. Bake 35 minutes at 375 degrees.

***Note:* Be sure to have an adult show you how to use a knife, stove, and oven safely.**

Winter

Visit a fresh produce market. If possible, find one that sells foods from different cultures. Learn which vegetables are winter vegetables. Try this recipe at a winter sleep-over or a winter solstice party.

Activity:

Jamaican Red Bean Stew

Ingredients:

- 2 cups* small red beans (canned, or use fresh ones after covering with water and soaking overnight)
- 3 medium carrots, diced
- 1 medium yam, diced
- 2 medium winter squash, diced
- 1-1/2 quarts* water
- 4 scallions, thinly sliced
- 2 cups* light coconut milk (canned)
- 2 tablespoons* fresh thyme, chopped
- 2 cloves garlic, minced
- salt and (hot) pepper to taste

Directions:

1. Place beans and water in a large pot.
2. Bring to boil, reduce heat, then cover and simmer for 45 minutes or until tender.
3. Add carrots, yam, squash, and coconut milk.
4. Bring to boil again, reduce heat, cover and simmer until vegetables are soft, about 15 minutes.
5. Add scallions and spices. Simmer uncovered until stew thickens.
6. Enjoy with freshly baked bread.

* See page 208 for the metric conversion chart.

A Year's Worth of Healthy Eating

Celebrate the Girl Scout birthday on March 12th with a "Girl Scouts Are Healthy" party! Have foods that make up each of the rows of the Food Guide Pyramid in the right proportions. Each of you can bring your favorite food. Plan in advance who is bringing what so that all your dishes make up a complete pyramid.

Boost Your Immune System

A healthy immune system helps you stay well during the cold and flu season. Follow these five suggestions for a strong defense:

1. Go to bed an hour earlier, especially if you feel as if you're coming down with a cold.
2. Wash your hands several times a day, especially if someone in your family is sick.
3. Try eating a green, leafy vegetable like collard greens, kale, or broccoli rabe.
4. Try a new flavor of yogurt. The good bacteria in yogurt protects the immune system.
5. Drink six to eight 8-ounce* glasses of water every day, more when you are sweating a lot.

Safety Alert! Bacteria that come from food can grow quickly in hot temperatures. Don't leave food sitting out longer than an hour. Keep refrigerated foods cold until you're ready to eat.

During summer, outdoor fun is celebrated across America. With pool or beach parties taking place, no one wants to be inside cooking. Plan a "cookless" healthy meal, or cook outdoors on a grill. Grilling vegetables brings out the natural sugars inside them, making vegetables taste yummy!

Note: An adult should handle the grilling, but you can prepare the veggies.

Vegetables to grill: asparagus, broccoli, cherry tomatoes, eggplant, green pepper, mushrooms, onions, potatoes, and more. You can even grill fruit! Try grilling peaches, nectarines, or bananas. Yum!

What You Do

1. Wash vegetables.
2. Slice vegetables into bite-sized pieces.
3. Brush with oil to prevent sticking to the grill.
4. Put vegetables on a skewer or in a grill basket if available.
5. Most vegetables take only 8 to 10 minutes to grill.

A Great Summer Drink:

Chocolate Fruit Smoothie

- 1 cup* low-fat milk
- 4 tablespoons* instant powdered milk
- 2 tablespoons* cocoa powder
- 3 tablespoons* sugar
- 1 cup* frozen pitted cherries, raspberries, or strawberries

OR

- 2 cups* fresh pitted cherries, raspberries, or strawberries

Mix in a blender until smooth and enjoy. Serves four.

* See page 208 for the metric conversion chart.

Food Facts

Some foods are processed. That means they have been changed in some way from their natural state. These foods usually come in boxes or cans, and they may have chemicals added to them to make the foods taste better or stay fresher longer.

Many food products today are also artificially (not naturally) flavored to taste sweeter. Some are artificially colored to look more attractive. Did you know that each American eats or drinks about five pounds* of chemical additives a year?!

Food Labels to the Rescue!

How can you tell when artificial "stuff" has been added to your foods? By learning how to read food labels! All those added products, such as food coloring and artificial sweeteners, are listed on the food labels.

Labels provide a lot of information. Ingredients are listed in order from "most" to "least." For example, if sugar is listed as the first ingredient, then that product contains more sugar than anything else. Did you know that fructose, sucrose, dextrose, molasses, corn syrup, and honey are all forms of sugar?

Activity:

Compare Food Labels

Collect labels from the cans and boxes of a variety of products. Bring them to your Girl Scout meeting. Copy down the following information from each label:

Nutrition Facts

Total calories	
	% Daily Value
Protein	
Calories from fat	
Vitamin A	
Sodium	
Vitamin C	
Dietary fiber	
Calcium	
Sugars	
Iron	

Compare the labels and look for the products that have the healthiest ingredients. Don't forget to look at the suggested serving sizes, too. How much of each food do you have to eat to take in the amounts listed on the label? Which foods are highest in fiber? Which foods have the most vitamins and minerals, such as calcium and potassium? Which foods are lowest in sodium (salt) and fat?

Discuss with your troop how this information can help you make food choices.

* See page 208 for the metric conversion chart.

Learn to Survive Stress

Imagine this:

You just discovered that your piano teacher has scheduled a big recital in two months. You feel totally unprepared, and *very* nervous about performing in front of a crowd for the first time.

Or this: You suddenly realize that your social studies project is due on Monday morning. It's now Sunday night.

Or this: You feel like one of your closest friends is drifting away, becoming closer to a new group of kids. You can't stop worrying about losing her friendship.

Stress is the way your body or mind reacts to people or situations that put demands on you physically, mentally, or emotionally. Some stress can be helpful in your work, play, and exercise. For example, positive stress is the feeling you have before your birthday party—a bit nervous but also ready and excited. But, more often, stress can be negative. That's why learning how to manage stress is a useful skill.

Do More

Check out the "Stress Less" badge in the *Junior Girl Scout Badge Book* for more activities about reducing stress.

Stress Less

Managing Stress

Use these ideas to manage stress:

- Face up to what's causing the stress.
- Express your feelings.
- Talk it over with someone you trust.
- Think about good things.
- Work with others to solve problems.
- Take a break!
- See if there's a way to reorganize things.
- See if there's another way to look at things that will help you accept them.
- Know that you can learn and grow from your mistakes.
- Treat your mind and body right: relax, exercise, sleep, and eat well.
- Get involved in another activity—a hobby, sport, or service project, for example.

Responses That Don't Reduce Stress

Though you might be tempted to do some of these things when you are stressed, DO NOT:

- Ignore your feelings.
- Try to deal with it all by yourself.
- Just wish that it would go away by itself.
- Blame yourself.
- Think about only the bad things.
- Think that you're supposed to be perfect.
- Think that everything is wrong and needs to change.
- Treat your body badly with cigarettes, alcohol, drugs, undereating, or overeating.

Read More

See the "Create and Invent" and "Explore and Discover" chapters in this handbook for hobby ideas that will help you manage your stress. The "Adventures in Girl Scouting" chapter has some great service project ideas. And of course you can find information earlier in this chapter about many fun sports activities.

Finding Time

Managing your time, like managing your money, is a skill you can learn. The trick is to figure out the things you *must* do and the things you *want* to do and then try to squeeze in a few other things! Then you have to *prioritize,* which means to arrange everything on your list in order of importance.

Make a list of all the things you did this week. Include everything! There was school, of course. What did you do at home? Do chores? Watch TV? Play games with family members? Do homework? Practice an instrument? What about time away from home? Did you play sports? Spend time with friends? Go to religion class? Attend a party or dance? Make your list as complete as possible.

Now examine your list and:

1. Put an X next to all the things you had to do. For example, you had to sleep and study.

2. Put a smiley face next to the things that made you feel happy.

3. Put a star next to the things that made you feel close to your family.

4. Put a heart next to the things that exercised your body.

5. Put a frown next to the things you did not like to do and did not have to do.

Look over your list. What kinds of activities are you doing the most? Are your activities balanced? What do you want to do more often, but don't have enough time to do? If you love to exercise, but can't fit it in, maybe you could spend less time doing other things (watching TV, hanging out) a few days a week.

Don't Wait Until It's Too Late!

Procrastination happens when you put off doing what you have to do. It's a bad habit many people share. For example, on Monday you find out you have a social studies test on Thursday. You'll have to study your notes and read four chapters in your textbook. But Thursday seems a long time away, so on Monday night you chat on the phone with your girlfriend and watch television until 10:00 p.m. On Tuesday, your mom asks you to watch your younger brother after school. You feel you need a reward after that (he wasn't quiet for a second!), so once your mom gets home you go to your girlfriend's house to listen to music and practice some dance moves. Now it's Wednesday and the test is tomorrow. No more procrastinating! Worse than that, now you feel stressed because you have so much studying to do. What would have been a better way to prepare for the test?

Here are a few ways you could have managed your time better to prepare for the test:

1. You could have broken the work into sections and studied a little bit each day.
2. You could have divided the work in half and studied Tuesday and Wednesday.
3. You could have made notes to study while on the bus, standing on line somewhere, or during other free moments.

Make a Plan

Here is a simple way to manage your time:

1. Make a list of what you need to get done. Your list could be for an evening, a day, or a week.
2. Put a star next to those things that are most important. Do those things first.
3. As you finish each thing on your list, cross it off. You'll feel good when you see how much you have accomplished.

Now you are all set to take advantage of your time as a Junior Girl Scout!

Procrastination Police!

Make a pact with some friends to try to help each other cut back on procrastinating. Get together and write down all of your "favorite" ways to procrastinate: talking on the phone, going shopping, playing video games, exercising. Make copies of the list for each of your friends. Next time you see a friend doing something on the list to procrastinate, gently remind her of your pact. (She will do the same thing for you.) Procrastination police to the rescue!

7 Let's Get Outdoors

In This Chapter You Will Learn About:

You have so much to do as a Junior Girl Scout, that sometimes it's hard to decide what to do next! That's certainly the case when you and a group are planning an outdoor activity:

- Should you have a cookout in the park or visit the zoo?
- Should you go horseback riding or take a bike trip?
- Should you learn how to paddle a canoe or go ice skating?
- Should you plan a campout at a council camp or state park?

The choices could go on and on. Luckily for you, as a Junior Girl Scout you can take part in many outdoor activities like these. With the help of a Girl Scout leader and other adults, the teamwork of other Girl Scouts, and the information in this chapter, you will be on your way to a lifetime of outdoor adventures.

As you learn about camping, don't forget to explore the possibilities at your Girl Scout council's summer events and day camp or resident camp for great summer fun!

Stay Safe

Here's how to make sure your outdoor adventure is safe.

1. Review the book *Safety-Wise* with your leader and group for the checkpoints that relate to the activity you are going to do.

2. Get your permission slips signed by your parent or guardian and notify your leader of any medical concerns you might have, such as an allergy to bee stings.

3. Talk to someone who has visited or knows the outdoor place you plan to go. For example, you might want to know whether there is a bathroom, clean drinking water, and a place to buy food or supplies nearby. You might have questions about the terrain (is the site hilly?) or the plants and animals (are there any to avoid?).

4. Decide in your group what type of clothing you will wear or bring. Athletic shoes and socks will be good footwear for most outings when you will be doing lots of walking.

5. Make sure you are physically fit. If you plan to hike or bicycle, get in shape so you can really enjoy it!

6. Learn about symptoms and first aid treatment for emergencies in hot and cold temperatures. (See the "How to Stay Safe" chapter in this handbook.) This might be the time to start earning the "First Aid" badge in the *Junior Girl Scout Badge Book.*

7. Carry your own water and drink regularly to avoid getting dehydrated. This is especially important when you are working hard or when it is hot. Only drink water that you know is from a safe source, like a city or county water supply. (Any water from lakes or streams must be purified before drinking to kill germs that could make you sick.)

8. Learn the buddy system and look out for your buddy's safety. Always have a plan to follow if you get separated from the group.

Your Planning steps

step 1

The first step in planning for any outdoor activity is deciding where to go and what to do when you get there. The *Junior Girl Scout Badge Book* and this handbook will give you plenty of ideas. You can come up with tons of other ideas by brainstorming with your group.

step 2

In a meeting or two you can plan a hike or a day trip. You might need to make telephone calls to find out about places. Get maps and brochures that tell you:

- How far away the place is
- When it is open
- What special programs are offered

step 3

Use these questions to help you plan the trip:

Who is going?
What will we do?
When will we go?
What will it cost?
What do we need to take?
How will we get there?

Make Your HIKE FUN!

If you want to take a hike, there are a zillion and one ways to do it. Choose a hike from this list or create your own!

A-B-C hike. Find a plant or animal starting with each letter of the alphabet.

Career hike. Keep track of how many careers you see as you pass people who are working.

Water-cycle hike. Look for parts of the water cycle as you hike: precipitation (rain, snow, fog); evaporation (sunlight, dried puddles); run-off (water moving on the ground, storm drains); bodies of water (lake, ocean); flowing water (streams, rivers).

Throw-away hike. Pick up objects (like fall leaves and dried grasses) as you walk. Make a collage with them.

Food-chain hike. Take notes on the food chains you see in action as you observe plants and animals that depend upon each other for food. Try for three to five links, then start over with a new chain. One chain, for example, could be: soil, grass, bug, sparrow, hawk.

Habitat hike. Look for homes of animals in the wild.

Picture-story hike. Stop every ______ yards, blocks, or feet (fill in the blank yourself) and frame a picture with your hands. Write a sentence about what you see. Then read all your sentences at the end of the hike.

Math-in-nature hike. Find the following shapes while hiking: circle, square, hexagon, spiral, diamond, triangle, ellipse (oval).

Soundless hike. Hike a forest trail without making noise or talking.

Follow-the-leader-hike. Set up a trail for another group to follow. Use trail marker symbols to show the way.

Rainbow hike. Look for as many different colors as you can find.

What to Pack for a Day Trip

What do you put in your day pack? What would you carry in your day pack for a hike in the city? What about a hike in the woods? Here are some of the basic items you will need.

Map
Or bring a schedule if you are taking public transportation.

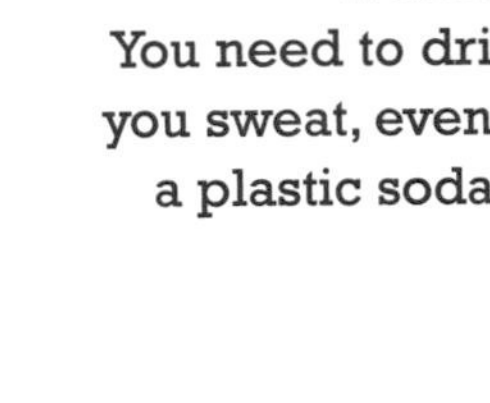

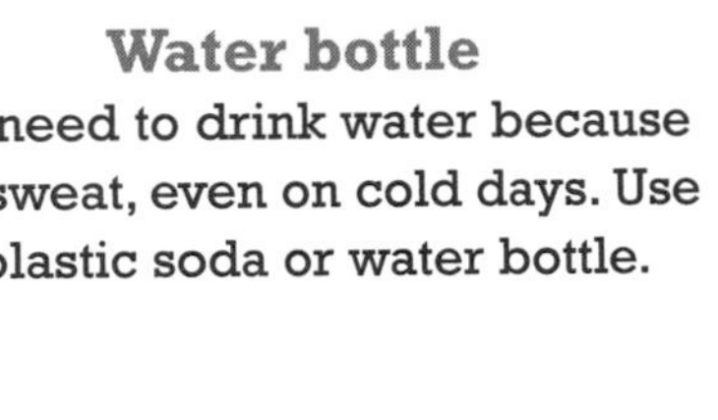

Water bottle
You need to drink water because you sweat, even on cold days. Use a plastic soda or water bottle.

Portable snack
This could include a granola bar, an apple, a piece of hard candy, or "gorp," which can give you a quick surge of energy. (See the recipe for gorp on the next page.) You might also need to bring your lunch.

Emergency kit
You need to have coins or a phone card for emergency phone calls, along with emergency phone numbers.

Rain gear
This can be a poncho, or a rain jacket and rain pants. Be prepared!

Pencil and paper

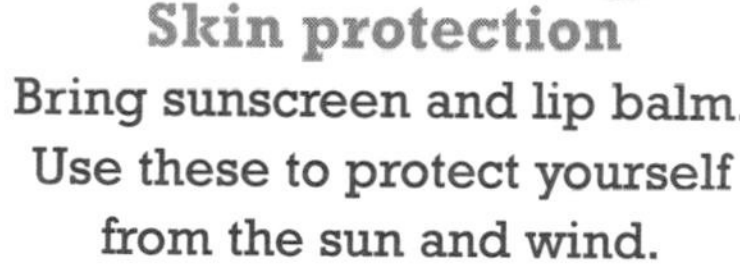

Skin protection
Bring sunscreen and lip balm. Use these to protect yourself from the sun and wind.

Pocket mirror
A small mirror can be used for signaling if you get lost.

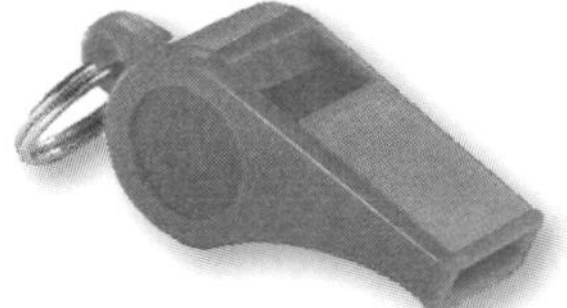

Whistle
Use this if you get lost or separated from the group. It saves energy and stress in a scary situation.

GOOD OLD RAISINS PEANUTS

GORP

Recipe for Gorp

- 1/2 cup* roasted or boiled peanuts (make sure no one has a peanut allergy)
- 1/2 cup* sunflower seeds
- 1/2 cup* raisins
- 1/2 cup* chocolate chips
- 1/2 cup* chopped dried fruit
- 1 cup* unsugared dry cereal (not flakes)

* See page 208 for the metric conversion chart.

It's Time to Learn Camping Skills!

After you have gone on a few trips close to home, and after you have planned and done a few outdoor activities, you will be ready to plan a camping trip. In addition to reading this chapter, check out the "Camp Together" badge in the *Junior Girl Scout Badge Book* to get you started.

Your leader or an adult from your council who is trained in camping and outdoor activities will help you. Outdoor flag ceremonies, a Girl Scouts' Own, and special evening campfire programs can all be a part of your camping experience.

Here are some of the outdoor skills you need in order to have a GREAT campout.

Dress for the Outdoors

"Be Prepared" is the best guide for choosing outdoor clothing. Always hope for the best in weather, but prepare for the worst. Check off the items on this list that you will need for your trip:

- ☐ underwear
- ☐ long pants (cotton/wool)
- ☐ shorts
- ☐ T-shirts
- ☐ long-sleeved shirts
- ☐ sweaters and sweatshirts
- ☐ long underwear (top and bottom)
- ☐ socks
- ☐ bandannas
- ☐ sleepwear
- ☐ sturdy shoes/hiking boots
- ☐ sneakers
- ☐ bathing suit
- ☐ sun hat
- ☐ wool hat
- ☐ gloves
- ☐ jacket
- ☐ rain coat and pants
- ☐ personal hygiene items: soap and shampoo, towel, washcloth, toothbrush, toothpaste, comb and brush
- ☐ prescription medication
- ☐ sewing repair kit
- ☐ sunscreen
- ☐ lip balm
- ☐ insect repellent

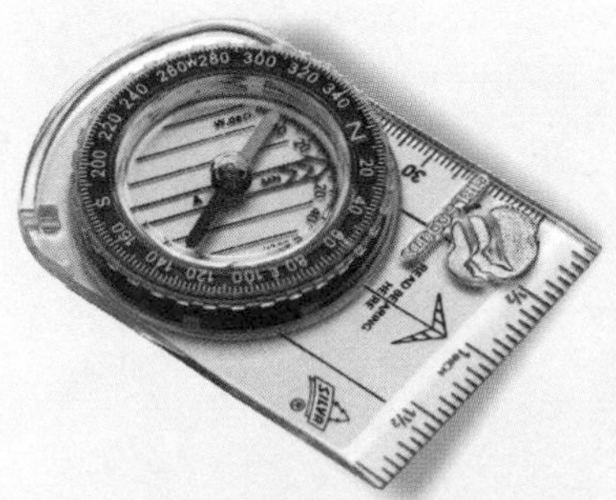

Find Your Way

Practice the compass, pacing, and map skills that appear in this chapter. You will need them to find your way to the campsite or to explore when you get there.

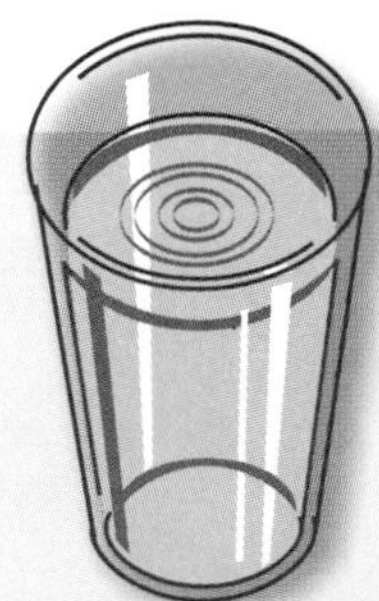

Know How to Get Water

You will need clean water for cooking, drinking, and washing (dishes and you!). Find out from your leader if there will be a water faucet available at the campsite. If not, you will need to be able to purify water. Your leader will help you learn this skill.

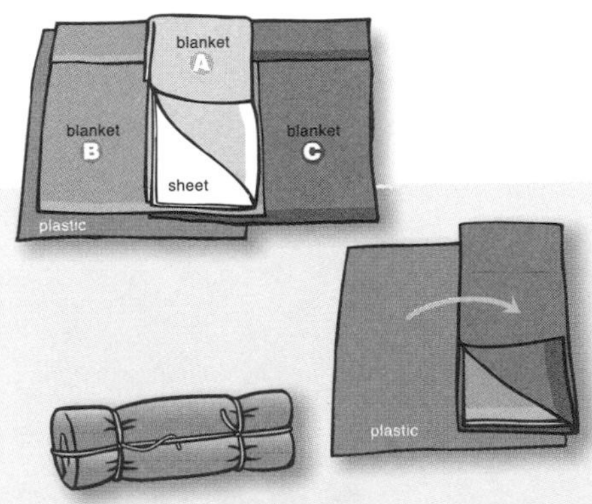

Pack Your Gear

Learn how to make a neat bedroll, or pack a sleeping bag so it won't come apart when you carry it. You will need to figure out how to pack all your things into a backpack or duffel bag. Put things into plastic bags first to keep them organized and dry.

And Don't Forget to:

- Make arrangements for the site (such as reservations if needed)
- Sign up adults to help you on the trip
- Make transportation arrangements
- Create a schedule of activities you want to do
- Create a kaper chart
- Get your parent/guardian permission slips signed

Other Important Items to Pack in Your Duffel Bag or Backpack

- [ ] sleeping bag/bedroll and plastic ground cloth
- [ ] water bottle
- [ ] first aid kit (see "How to Stay Safe" chapter in this handbook for details)
- [ ] flashlight
- [ ] extra batteries and bulb
- [ ] compass
- [ ] whistle
- [ ] mess kit: plate, cup, bowl, eating utensils
- [ ] nylon mesh bag for dishes
- [ ] notebook and pencil
- [ ] miscellaneous (such as money, maps, games)

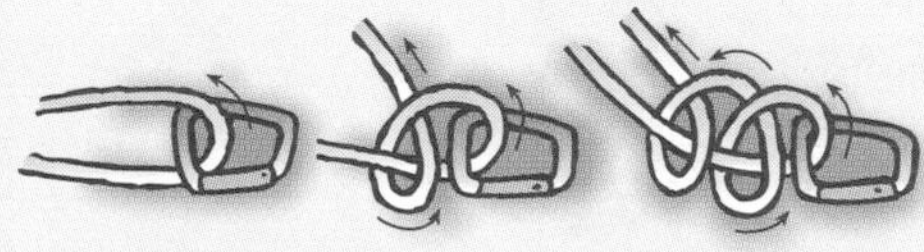

Tie Knots

Practice the knots that appear in this chapter before you go. See how many you can use while you are camping. Use cord and several knots to tie up your bedroll.

Cook Outdoors

With your group, plan the menus for your trip. Use simple recipes that will be fun and easy to cook outdoors. (Look at the "Be Healthy, Be Fit" chapter for nutrition hints.) A one-pot meal can make enough for everyone. Check out the recipe for Vegetarian Chili in this chapter.

Protect the Environment

Later in this chapter you will learn how to leave a campsite the same way you found it.

Cooking Outdoors

Whether you are cooking on a backyard barbecue or on a portable camp stove, you will need:

- A cool, dry place to store food
- A safe place to operate your stove or to build your fire
- A place to wash your hands
- A place to fix your food
- A place to eat
- A method for cleaning up
- A place to put garbage and items to be recycled

SOME OUTDOOR COOKING TIPS

1. One-pot meals are the easiest to fix and clean up.
2. Boiling water can be used to make many things: gelatin, hot cocoa, soup, pasta, vegetables, instant meals.
3. Dry foods, such as jerky, dried fruits, and rice, keep well without refrigeration.
4. Meat and dairy products spoil the most quickly, and need to be kept in a refrigerated place.
5. Use plastic bags and reusable containers to carry food. Buy food in bulk and repackage for travel.
6. Soap the outside of the pot when cooking on a fire. It will be much easier to clean later.
7. Learn to use cooking tools correctly. When you use a paring knife, hold the handle with your whole hand. Always cut away from you. Do not hold onto the blade. Keep at least an arm's length away from others when using a paring knife. Do not walk around while using it. Practice using a knife to cut an apple on a cutting board. Then try items like carrots that are a little harder.

Activity:

Make Vegetarian Chili

Try making this stew over a fire or stove. You need one large pot. Serves four to six.

What You Need

- 1 cup* uncooked rice
- 1 6-oz.* can tomato paste
- 2 cubes low-salt chicken or vegetable bouillon
- 2 12-oz.* cans red kidney beans
- 1 medium onion (chopped)
- 3 stalks of celery (chopped)
- 1 medium green or red pepper (seeded and chopped)
- 1 tablespoon* oil
- 3 carrots (peeled or scrubbed, and chopped)
- 1 tablespoon* chili powder
- 4 cups* water

What You Do

1. Sauté (fry) the onion and green pepper in the oil until soft.
2. Add celery and carrots and sauté for 2-3 minutes.
3. Add beans with liquid, chili powder, 4 cups* of water, tomato paste, and bouillon cubes.
4. Simmer.
5. Add rice.
6. Cook until rice is done: 20 minutes for white rice and 50 minutes for brown rice.

* See page 208 for the metric conversion chart.

Using a Camp Stove

A two-burner gas stove is a great way to cook when camping. It is fast and saves firewood.

Before You Camp

1. Read the directions for operating your particular stove and try it out to cook a simple snack or hot drink before you go.
2. Know what kind of fuel your stove needs. Plan to take extra fuel.
3. Gather all the equipment you will need for camp-stove cooking:
   - Pots
   - Potholders or mitts
   - Wooden matches
   - Safety equipment (water bucket, baking soda, or a portable fire extinguisher)
   - First aid kit

   Take a funnel if you are using gas fuel.
4. Review the Outdoor Cooking section of the book *Safety-Wise* before using the camp stove.

When Cooking

1. Always have an adult present.
2. Tie back your hair and do not wear loose or plastic clothing.
3. Find a safe, level spot outdoors for your stove.
4. Clear any debris away from around the stove.
5. Set up the stove in a place that is not windy. If the stove has a windscreen, put it in place to break the wind.
6. Never use the stove in a tent or indoors. This is dangerous because stoves can give off carbon monoxide, a gas that is harmful to people. It is also dangerous to have any type of flame inside a tent.
7. Read the operating instructions again and light the stove according to directions. Hold the match so the flame burns upward.
8. Do not reach over the stove. When stirring, hold onto the pan with a mitt. On a small, single-burner stove, take the pot off the stove before stirring and then return it.
9. Adjust the flame for cooking. Blue flame is the hottest. You might want to coat the outside bottom of your pans with soap before placing them over the flame, so pot scrubbing is easier.
10. Do not leave the stove unattended. If you run out of fuel, never refuel while it is hot.
11. When you are finished cooking, let the stove cool before cleaning it. Make sure that gas valves are all tightly turned off before packing.

Activity:

Hot Fruit Dessert

Make a solar oven from corrugated cardboard and aluminum foil. Put your food into a black pot with a lid, and place it inside a plastic roasting bag. Put the bag into the solar oven in an area where the oven will be heated by the sun for several hours.

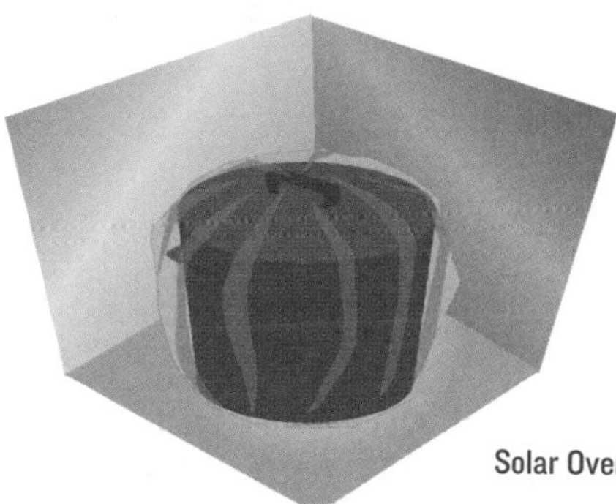

Solar Oven

Here's an easy recipe to try:

- 3 bananas
- 4 apples
- Lemon
- Water
- 3 teaspoons* cinnamon
- 6 whole cloves
- Honey, to taste (or sprinkle of sugar)

Squeeze juice from half a lemon into a bowl of water. Slice the bananas. Cut apples into eighths (peel if desired) and place apples into lemon water to keep them from discoloring. Drain apples. Mix fruit, cinnamon, cloves, and honey. Place mixture in a black pot and cover with tight fitting lid. Cook for 1 to 1-1/2 hours in solar oven. Serves four to six people.

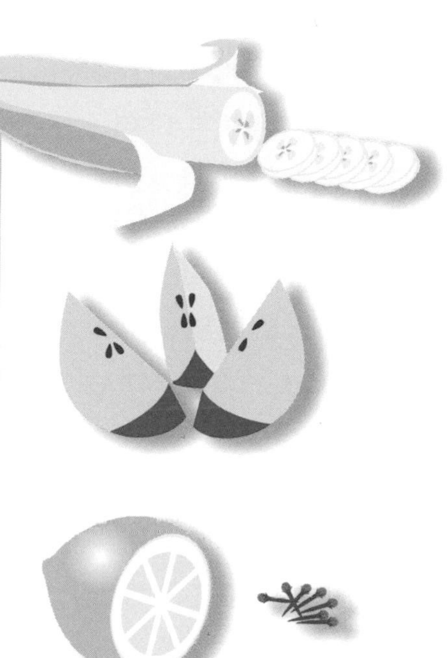

Activity:

Solar Noodle Cookies

- 6 oz.* chocolate chips
- 6 oz.* butterscotch chips
- 1 large can chow mein noodles

Melt the chips using the sun by putting them in a dark or black pan. When they are almost melted, stir them until the melting is almost complete. Add the noodles and mix well. Drop by spoonful onto a sheet of waxed paper. Eat when cool. Makes approximately 30 pieces.

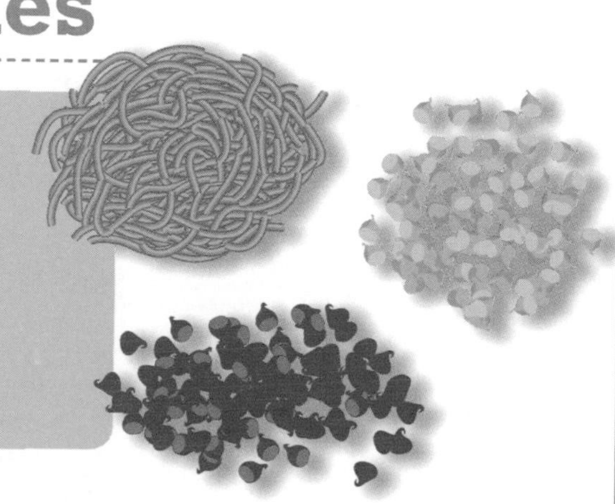

* See page 208 for the metric conversion chart.

Build a Fire

Girl Scouts learn how to make fires because it is a useful skill to have in the outdoors. Some campsites and parks don't allow fires because not enough wood is available, or because there is a fire danger or too much air pollution. If this is true where you are camping, think about other ways to cook, or plan meals that don't require cooking!

Before You Make a Fire

A fire needs fuel and air to burn. You need three sizes of wood in order to make a fire that will last.

TINDER

is thin material that burns as soon as it is lit with a match. Tinder could be dry twigs, dry leaves, or wood shavings.

KINDLING

is larger in diameter than tinder, thin enough to catch fire before the tinder burns out, and large enough to help the fuel to light. Kindling is about the same diameter as your thumb and should be dry enough to snap when you break it.

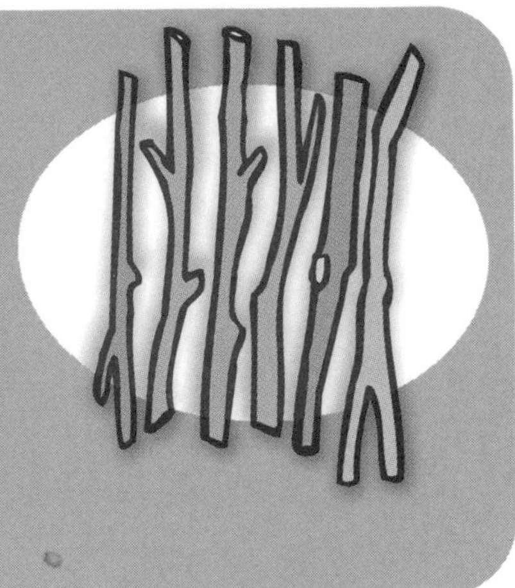

FUEL

is thicker pieces of wood that keep a fire going. Fuel should be dry, seasoned wood found on the ground or in a woodpile. Have enough tinder, kindling, and fuel on hand so you do not have to leave your fire once you start it.

Where to Build

Use an established fireplace or fire ring. A fire ring is an area of bare soil that will contain the fire. It should be an area without roots, dry materials, and overhanging branches.

How to Build

1. Make a small triangle with three pieces of kindling, leaving an air space under the top bar of the triangle.

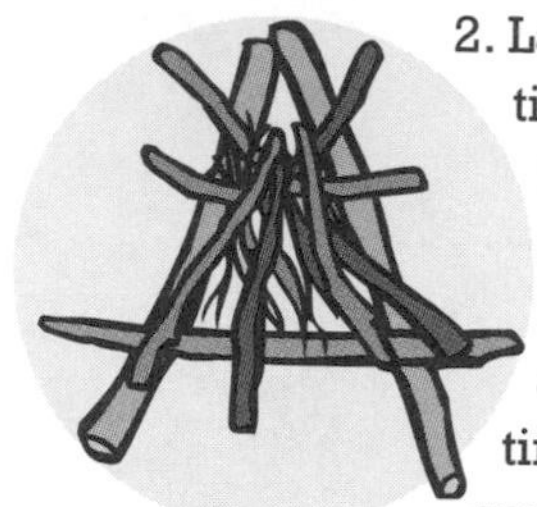

2. Lay a handful of tinder against the apex (top) of the triangle, leaving some air space. Lean tinder toward the center, upright. (You can also use a combination of tinder and a fire-starter.)
3. Strike a wooden match close to the tinder and away from your body. Hold the match under the tinder at ground level so the flame burns upward.
4. As the tinder catches, add additional tinder carefully, then begin placing kindling so it leans against the triangle above the flaming tinder. Continue adding kindling, building a cone shape.
5. Add fuel (large pieces of wood) to the fire so the kindling can catch it on fire. Leave air spaces, and use only the amount of fuel you need.

Make the fire small. Conserve fuel and avoid smoke pollution.

If you need a concentrated heat source (to boil water, for example), continue making the cone shape and cook over the flames. You might also use a grate to support your cooking pots. As the fire burns down, it forms coals. This is the best heat to cook on. Great for making s'mores!

SAFETY TIPS FOR FIRES

Being able to build a fire is a basic survival skill that provides heat for warmth and fuel for cooking. You might make a campfire with your troop or group, or with your family at a campground. Always check fire-making rules of the area, and follow these safety tips:

When You Are Making a Fire

1. Have a bucket of water and a shovel nearby before building your fire. You might need to smother the fire with dirt, or to stir wet coals when you put it out.
2. If you are building a fire in a fireplace, make sure the draft in the chimney is open and a screen is placed across the fireplace to prevent sparks from jumping out onto clothing or rugs.
3. Tie back your hair and wear long pants.
4. Do not start a fire outside during air-pollution alerts, high winds, or very dry conditions.

When You Are Finished

1. Let the fire die down until only ashes are left.
2. With a long stick or shovel, stir the ashes, sprinkle them with water, then stir again. Continue until there is no gray ash and the fire bed is cool. Pouring water on a fire can cause steam and rock explosions.
3. Remove any signs that you were there, returning the site to the way you found it. If you've used a fireplace, leave it clean by removing the ashes. Ask the site manager what you should do with the ashes.

Using a Compass

Orienting arrow

Magnetic needle

Direction of travel arrow

A compass has a small, *magnetized needle* inside the compass housing that floats in air, water, or oil. The needle (red end) will always turn to the magnetic north of the earth. When you know where north is, you can find any other direction. You need a compass, preferably similar to the one pictured here, which has a *transparent base* for map reading.

The *compass housing* is marked with the 360 degrees of a circle. North, east, south, and west are the four main (or cardinal) points on the compass. Look at the housing and find the degree reading for each of the *cardinal points*. (*Hint:* North is at 0° or 360°. East is ____. South is ____. West is ____.)

Hold the compass in front of you at waist height, with the *direction-of-travel arrow* pointing straight ahead of you. To find north, turn the compass housing until 0° is lined up with the direction-of-travel arrow. Slowly turn your body until the red magnetic arrow is pointing in the same direction as the *orienting arrow* in the bottom of the compass. When this happens, you are facing north.

To travel to the north, follow the direction-of-travel arrow carefully with your eyes and look into the distance. Look for a landmark, like a tree or a rock, in your line of sight. Walk to that object, then line up your red magnetic arrow with the orienting arrow again, sight an object, and continue walking. Try the same thing with other directions!

To travel back the way you came, add 180° to the degree reading on your direction-of-travel arrow by turning the compass housing by 180°. Turn your body so that the red magnetic arrow lines up with the orienting arrow, and follow your sighting along the direction-of-travel arrow.

Whenever you are facing north:

- **east is to your right**
- **west is to your left**
- **south is behind you**

Activity:

Where Are You? Part 1

Figure out the directions to several objects around you. See if your friends get the same readings if they are in the same place as you.

Find Your Pace

Pacing helps you measure distances as you walk. Once you know how to determine your pace, you can determine distances anywhere you can walk. A pace is defined as the length of two steps.

What You Need
A 50-foot or 100-foot* tape measure. (If you don't have a measuring tape, use string marked off in one-foot segments.)

What You Do

1. Mark off 100 feet* on a flat, level surface with the tape measure.
2. Walk the distance three times. Always start with your left foot. Count each time your right foot hits the ground as you walk.
3. Each time you finish walking the 100 feet,* write down the number of paces you counted.
4. Add up the three numbers and divide by three. The number you get is the average number of paces it takes for you to walk 100 feet.*

Example	Your Pacing
31 paces first time	_____ paces first time
+ 34 paces second time	+ ___ paces second time
+ 28 paces third time	+ ___ paces third time
= 93 total paces	= ____ total paces
Total paces ÷ 3 = 31	Total paces ÷ 3 = _____
(average number of paces)	(average number of paces)

5. Now divide your average number into 100 feet* to get the length of your pace.

Example	Your Pacing
100 ÷ 31 = 3.2 feet*	100 ÷ (your average number of paces) = (length of your pace) Write this number down here so you won't forget it. The length of my pace is ___________.

Why Your Pace Is Important

Now when you walk, you can count each time your right foot touches the ground and multiply this number by the length of your pace to get the distance you have walked.

Test Yourself

Learn to judge distances using your knowledge of pace and time. Walk a distance that you know to be one-half mile* at a comfortable pace. Time how long it takes you. Do this more than once and take an average. Use this knowledge to estimate how far you walk for an unknown distance.

* See page 208 for the metric conversion chart.

Activity:

Where Are You? Part 2

Start at a spot outdoors that you mark with a small rock or marker.

1. Set your compass to 40°.
   Walk ten paces in that direction.
2. Set your compass for 130°.
   Walk five paces in that direction.
3. Set your compass for 220°.
   Walk ten paces in that direction.
4. Set your compass to 310°.
   Walk five paces in that direction.

How close are you to your original starting spot?

Activity:

Where Are You? Part 3

Give your friends compass directions that will have them walking in the pattern of a square, a triangle, or a rectangle.

Read a Map

Maps help you get from one place to another. Maps can help you figure out where you are and how to get to a place you want to go. They can also help you to estimate distances. Some maps can tell you if you will be going up or downhill.

Being able to read a map is an important skill, whether you are traveling in a car, riding on a bus, or hiking in the woods. You can even learn how to read a weather map to see an approaching storm.

How to Practice Your Skills

1. Use your compass to orient a map. Place your compass near the north symbol on the map. Turn the map until the magnetic arrow in the compass is parallel to the north arrow on the map and pointing in the same direction.
2. Hold your thumb at the place where you are currently located. As you move, slide your thumb along the map slowly. If you do this correctly, you will always know where you are. This technique is called "thumbing" by people who do orienteering, which is a sport that uses compasses and maps to travel cross-country.

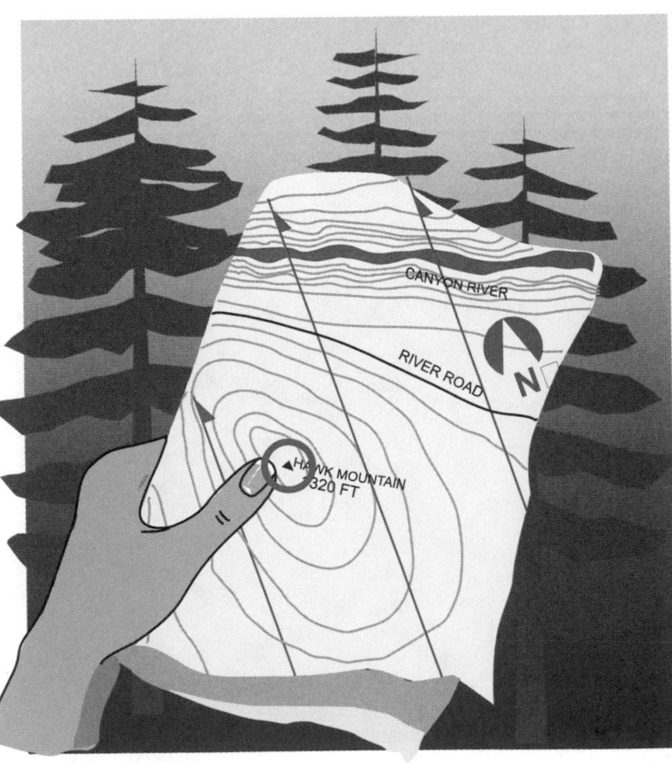

Activity:

Symbol Hunt

Find as many different kinds of maps as possible, including highway maps, bus maps, park maps, trail maps, topographic (elevation) maps, weather maps, and world maps. Look for different symbols that are listed in the map legends.

Here are some symbols you might find:

Freeway

Railroad

State Highway Patrol

Boat Landing

Paved Road

School

Roadside Rest Stop

Campground

Airport

Boat Launching Area

Tie Knots

Knots are used for tying bedrolls, doing macramé, and putting up a tent. Learn the basic knots shown here. Then challenge yourself to learn even more!

What You Need

- 2 pieces of clothesline or lightweight rope about 18 inches* long
- Bright-colored plastic tape

Tape the ends of the rope with the plastic tape to keep them from fraying.

Test Yourself

Decide which knot you would use to do each of the following.

- Anchoring a tent to a tent stake
- Tying a boat to a dock
- Shortening a clothesline
- Tying a rope to a leather dog leash

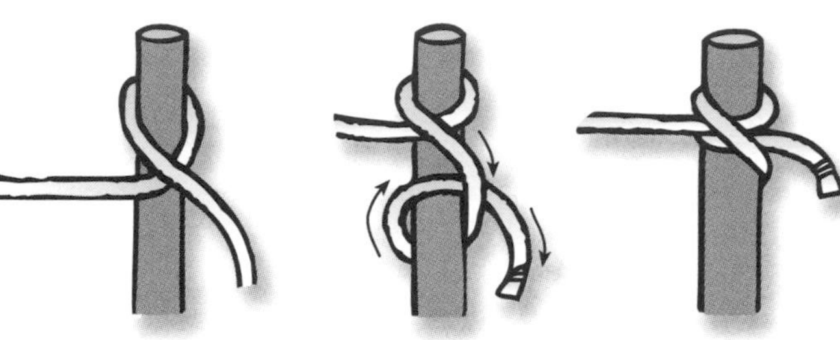

Clove Hitch
To fasten one end of a rope to a tree or post

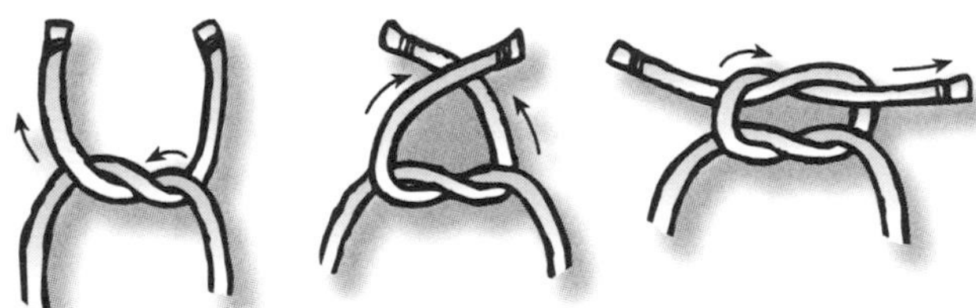

Square Knot
To join two cords of the same thickness

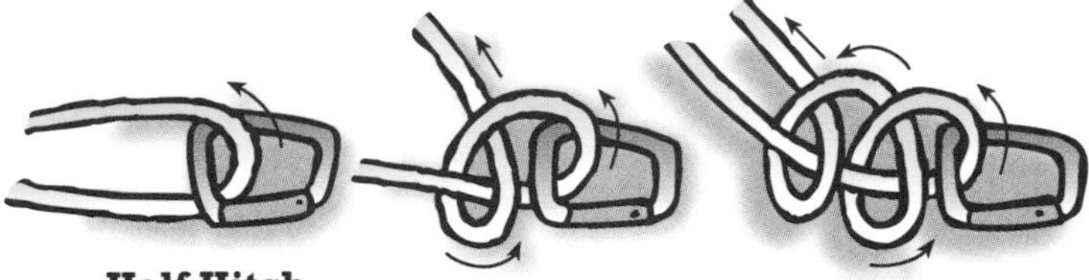

Half Hitch
To fasten a rope to a ring or tent stake

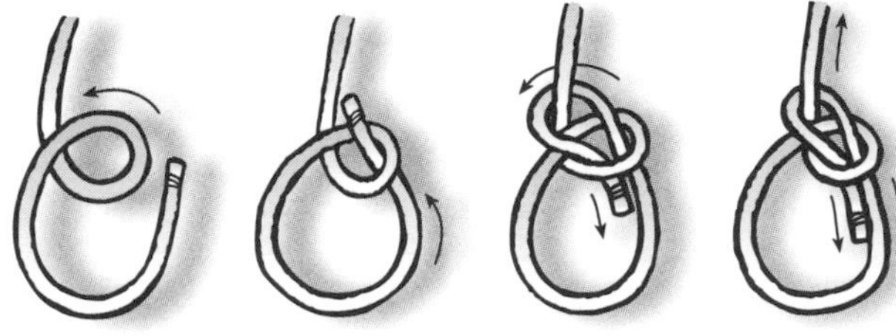

Bowline
To make a loop that won't slip

Tautline hitch
To make a loop that will slip when you want it to

* See page 208 for the metric conversion chart.

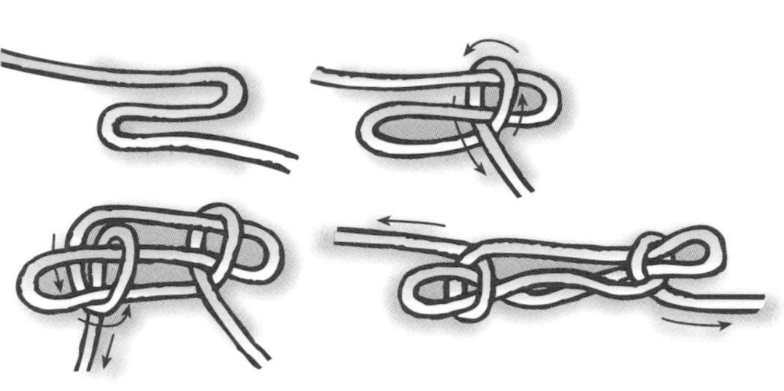

Sheepshank
To shorten a rope

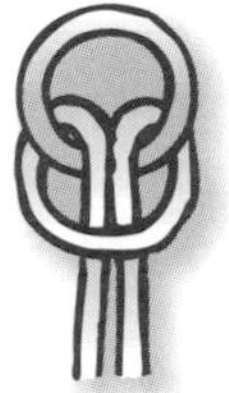
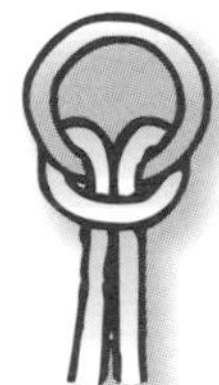

Lark's Head
To loop cord around a ring or hang your dish bag to a clothesline

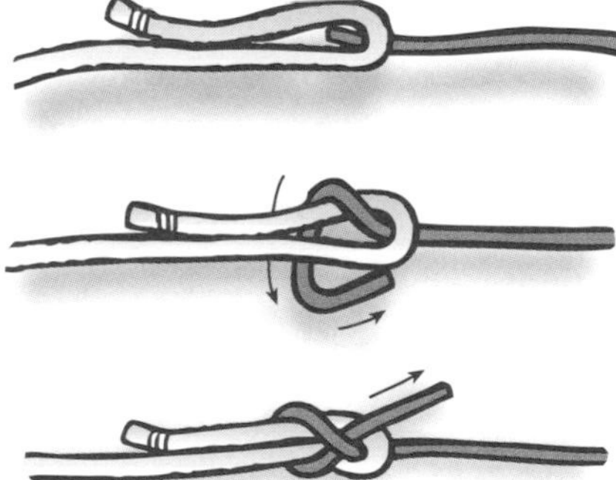

Sheetbend
To tie a thin rope to a thicker rope

Activity:

Knot-Tying Relay

Divide into teams. Each team gets two pieces of cord. Each team member in turn selects a piece of paper with the name of a knot written on it from a bag. The first person pulls out the name of a type of knot, ties it, and passes the cord and bag to the second person. That person unties the knot, picks out the name of another knot, and ties that knot. The game continues until each team member has tied a knot correctly.

Protect the Environment

Everything you do in the outdoors affects the environment in some way. The air you breathe, the water you swim in, and the soil you walk on are all part of the environment. Air, water, and soil, together with plants and animals, make up the *ecosystem* we live in.

Girl Scouts always use *minimal-impact skills* in order to leave the environment in the same shape they found it, or in better shape. Minimal-impact skills are actions you take to live in harmony with the environment. They are practiced everywhere in the outdoors: while picnicking in the park, hiking in the mountains, or snorkeling on an underwater coral reef.

What Can You Do?

When you conserve and use resources wisely, you keep something from being damaged or wasted. For example, you need to use water, but you can conserve it by taking short showers or turning the water off when you are brushing your teeth.

Here are other steps you can take to help the environment at home and at camp. Tell other people around you about these conservation efforts, too.

1. **Cut down on using cars for short trips.** Carpool with friends, use public transportation, ride your bike, or walk.
2. **Conserve water.** Help your family to fix leaky faucets, install a water saver in your shower, use a timer for showers, use the dishwasher only when full.
3. **Recycle or reuse items whenever possible.** Reuse shopping bags, buy recycled paper, participate in community recycling programs.
4. **Help keep air clean.** Don't burn trash. Plant trees to help filter the air.
5. **Help prevent soil erosion.** Stay on trails when hiking or walking so that you don't step on plants that hold soil in place. Avoid trails that go straight up and down hillsides. When it rains, the compacted soil washes down the hill. Help with a trail erosion project.

Give Some TLC

The environment needs some serious TLC (tender loving care). Noise, air, and water pollution are harming plants, animals, and people. The thinning ozone layer is leading to an increase in skin cancer. And global warming is causing severe droughts in some places and flooding in others.

The good news, however, is that young people just like you all over the world aren't waiting for someone else to fix things. They have made a commitment to help the planet by working on solutions to environmental problems in their own communities. And so can you!

Spot It, Solve It

Take a good look at your community. Are there things that you feel are harming the people, plants, or animals that live there? Here are some things to consider:

- Is garbage being dumped in a park or a vacant lot?
- Could you use more street trees to provide shade and oxygen?
- Does your school have a recycling program?
- Are people wasting water by planting and watering lawns?
- Do your neighbors use chemicals instead of natural methods to control pests in their homes and gardens?
- Are shoppers able to choose paper bags (which are recyclable) instead of plastic ones (which are not) at your supermarket?
- Has your city provided bicycle paths or racks so that people can bike to work or school?

Work on this challenge alone or with friends who want to help the environment as much as you do. Use the steps of the Action Plan in the "Adventures in Girl Scouting" chapter to help you.

Bite Off Only What You Can Chew

Pick one thing that you realistically can tackle. If you care enough about the environment, you will be able to make a difference, just like these kids.

An eleven-year-old girl was heartbroken that a developer was going to build houses on her favorite spot, a beautiful wetland. So she sprang into action. She found a local environmental protection law that kept the developer from destroying the wetland.

A group of fourth graders was worried about the pollution produced from the making of electricity. So they designed and installed switch plate covers with energy-saving messages and pictures in their school.

A nine-year-old girl noticed that the owls in her hometown were disappearing because they no longer had old buildings or trees in which to build their nests. She solved the problem by convincing her utility company to install telephone poles on her family's land so that she could place an owl nest box on each one.

Take a look around. What can you do?

Are You Environmentally Aware?

How much do you really know about *your* environment? Here are some things you can do to find out.

Activity:

Play Environment Expedition

Scientists are skilled observers. It takes practice to develop that skill. This game will help you sharpen your observation skills so that you will notice more things around you. Play this game outdoors with at least one other person. The person who checks off the most items on the list wins.

Find (but don't pick!):

The smallest animal ____
The biggest animal ____
The biggest tree ____
The smallest flower ____
A nest ____
A chewed leaf ____
Garbage ____
Water ____
An animal that flies ____
A plant growing on the sidewalk ____
A rock with two colors ____
A mushroom ____

Activity:

Tell Enviro-Riddles

Scientists are the all-time solvers of riddles. They use clues to find the answers to questions. Each clue leads to more details until the mystery is solved.

Create your own riddles to test how much your friends and family know about their environment. To do this, pick an animal or plant that lives in your community. Write down three to six clues about it. Put the hardest clue first and the easiest last.

Here's an example:

Clues

1. My mouth is in the middle of my body.
2. I have no legs, but I have many little "feet" under each of my arms.
3. I have no head, but I have an "eye" on the tip of each of my arms.
4. I live in the ocean and have five arms.
5. If I lose one of my arms, I can grow it back.

What Am I?

Read each clue to your friends and see if they can guess the answer before you tell them the last clue.

Answer: A sea star

Activity:

Do the Litter Bug

Don't worry, you won't be throwing candy wrappers and other litter on the street. *Litter* in this case is the name given to the layer of dead leaves found on the soil. And the *bug* refers to those creepy crawly things.

Why should you even care about little critters that live under leaves? A lot of them chomp on dead plants, so they're like an itty-bitty sanitation crew. That means you don't have to slog through tons of leaves each time you want to walk in the park or the woods.

What You Need

- A resealable plastic sandwich bag
- One white coffee filter
- Water
- A wide-mouth jar
- A large funnel
- A high-intensity lamp
- A magnifying glass

What You Do

1. Collect leaf litter from a park or your backyard any time of year except during the winter. Place it in the plastic bag and seal the bag until you get indoors.
2. Dampen the filter paper with water so the bugs won't dry out. Place it in the bottom of the jar. (The white color of the filter paper will make it easier for you to spot the animals when they drop from the funnel.)
3. Place the funnel on the jar. (The bigger the funnel, the better.)
4. Fill the funnel with leaf litter.
5. Place the lamp right over the funnel, but don't let the bulb touch the leaves. The heat will make the tiny animals move down to a cooler spot. (This may take up to 20 minutes, so be patient!)
6. Look at the animals that fall on the filter paper with your magnifying glass.
7. Return the leaves and the animals to where they belong as soon as you can.

8 Create and Invent

In This Chapter You Will Learn About:

Do you have a hobby? Maybe you like to work on projects to help the environment, like the kids in the "Let's Get Outdoors" chapter. Maybe you like to participate in sports and games, like the ones in the "Be Healthy, Be Fit" chapter. In this chapter you will learn about hobbies that let you create and invent.

When you are really involved in a hobby, you can lose track of time because you are so focused on what you are doing. When you are finished, you feel full of energy because you have been doing something you really enjoy.

Go Figure

What do the following have in common?

- Counting out money at the store
- Measuring windows for new curtains
- Tying knots
- Bettering your swim time

If you guessed that all of these things have something to do with math, you're right! Did tying knots throw you? Believe it or not, just as some mathematicians study shapes (geometry), other mathematicians and scientists study the relationship between the knotted and unknotted loops in many fields of science, such as chemistry.

Activity:

Geometry That Moves

What You Need

- Pen
- Ruler
- Compass for drawing circles
- Sheets of tracing paper

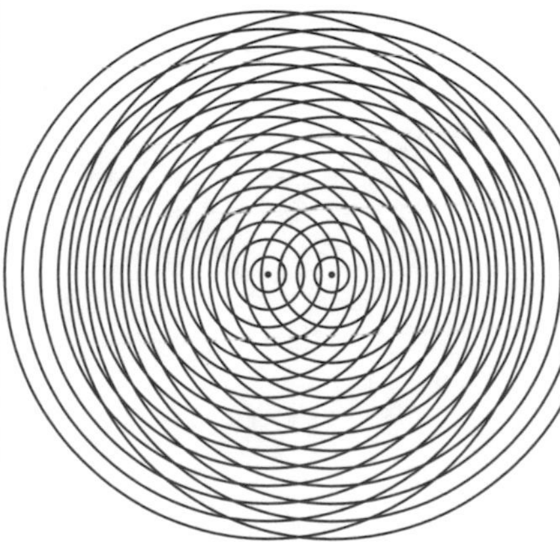

What You Do

1. In the center of a piece of tracing paper, construct a small (1/2 inch*) triangle, circle, square, or other geometric figure. Use a ruler for straight-line figures and a compass for circles.
2. Carefully draw the same figure outside the original, keeping lines parallel and as close as possible without touching. A space of 1/8 inch* is good, 1/16 inch* is even better.
3. Draw larger and larger figures until about half the white space in the paper is full.
4. Repeat the same process on a different sheet of paper. You can make the same or a different design. If you made a circle first, make a figure with straight lines on the second paper.
5. Place one design over the other and move the sheets around. What happens to the straight lines?

For a variation, try making patterns with string art. Tape small nails into a wooden board. (Read about tools later in this chapter.) Then lace fine string or thread around the nails to make patterns that seem to curve and wave.

How Does This Work?

Moiré patterns are all around you—once you realize what they are! These patterns are formed when you overlap materials with repeating lines. The repeating lines can be straight or circular. When one set of lines is placed over another and moved, a pattern is formed.

A simple moiré can be made by taking two hair combs with straight teeth and placing them one on top of the other so that the teeth line up. Now move the comb on top. The shimmery pattern you observe is a moiré.

Using moiré as a search word, go online and find other examples of moiré patterns. There are some wonderful sites where you can experiment with color, shapes, lines, and width of lines.

* See page 208 for the metric conversion chart.

Make a Friendship Anklet

Activity:

What You Need
- 6 yards* of twine per anklet
- Beads for decoration (optional)
- Heavy-duty tape to hold the twine taut

What To Do

1. Cut the twine into two pieces that are each 3 yards* long.

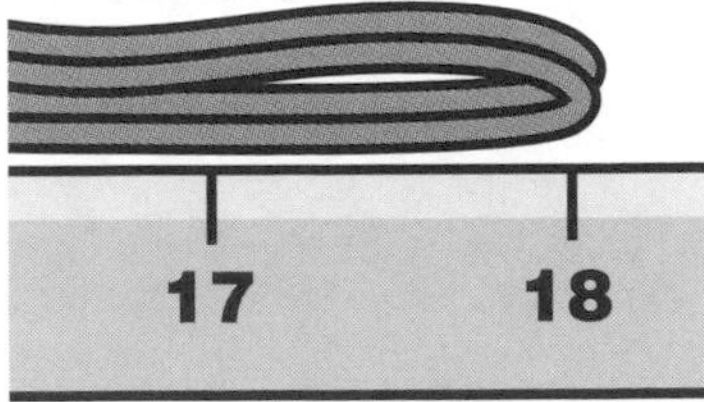

2. Fold both pieces 18 inches* from the end.

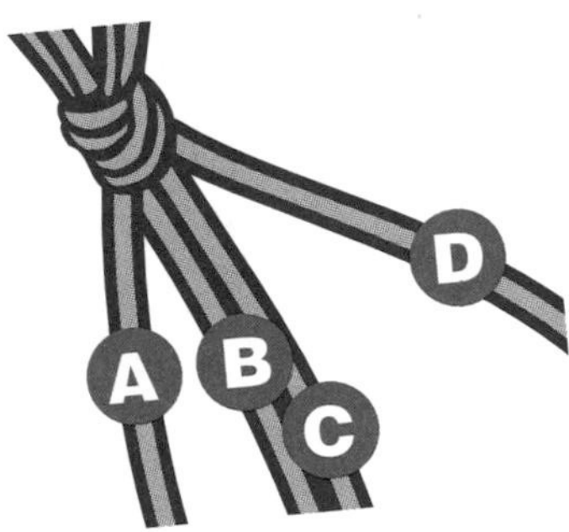

5. Tape the ends of the two 18-inch* pieces so that the twine is taut. The two 18-inch* pieces are strands B and C in the diagram.

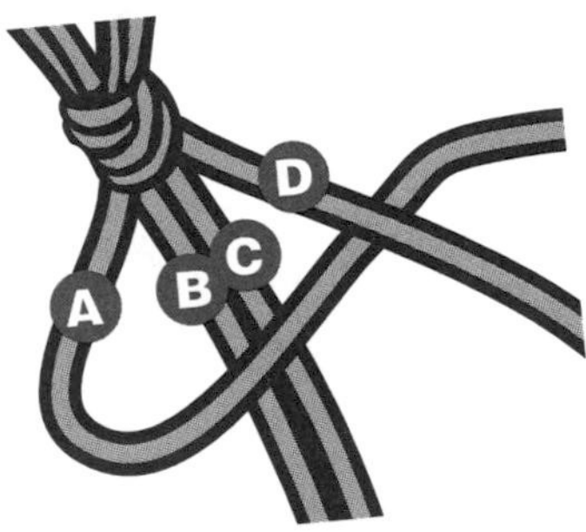

6. Cross A over B and C, and under D.

Note: A large clipboard or a piece of foam core or heavy cardboard can be used as a portable surface for making anklets and bracelets. This is an especially good activity to do on long car trips.

3. Hold the gathered ends together. You have two 18-inch* strands and two $7\frac{1}{2}$-foot* strands. Tie the ends together into a knot 4 inches* from the point where the strands are folded.

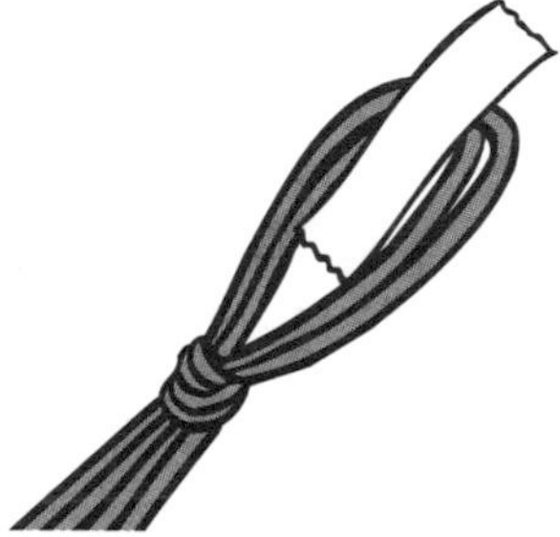

4. Tape the fold to a table or chair or other flat, steady surface.

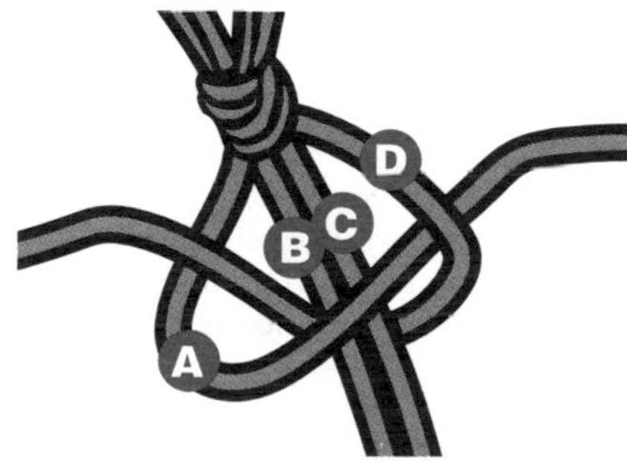

7. Bring D under B and C and then up through the loop made by A and pull tight. Repeat steps 6 and 7 until the anklet is the desired length.

8. Add beads wherever you want. You can put beads on one, two, three, or all four of the strands. When you have made your anklet long enough to fit around your ankle (with length left to tie the ends), make a knot that matches the top knot. Trim the twine and knot each of the four strands so the anklet doesn't fray.

* See page 208 for the metric conversion chart.

Practical Geometry

Do you have a bunch of old greeting cards with great designs? Instead of throwing them out, turn them into decorative boxes. You can give some away as gift boxes or swaps, or use them yourself as storage boxes for hair accessories, jewelry, etc. And you are doing the environment a favor by recycling!

Find This

Origami or a folded paper model is not only art but a geometric figure. Geometry is a part of mathematics that deals with points, lines, angles, surfaces, and solids. As you do this project, look for the shapes, lines, and points formed by your folding. At step 10, take your folded box apart before you glue it and lay the paper flat. What do you see? Now fold it back up and put those shapes and lines to work.

Activity:

What You Need

- Old greeting cards
- Scissors
- Glue (optional)
- Ruler

What You Do

1. Cut the card in half. The part with the picture or design will be the box top (the lid). The part with the greeting will be the box bottom.

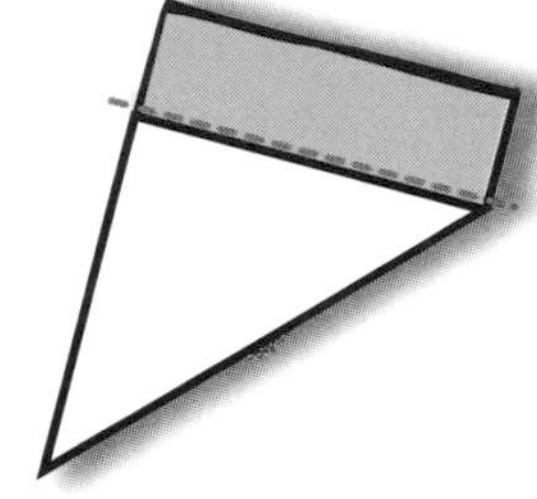

2. Fold the card top in half diagonally and cut along the line of paper left over. Unfold and you will have a square. *Note:* You can center your design first. The middle of your square will be the middle of your box top.

3. Using the top as your pattern, cut the bottom half of the card into a square about 1/8 inch* smaller all around.

Now you are going to turn these pieces of paper into a folded box.

4. Start with the bottom. Fold the paper in half diagonally, first one corner and then the other. Press on your folds to make sharp creases. Unfold back to your square.

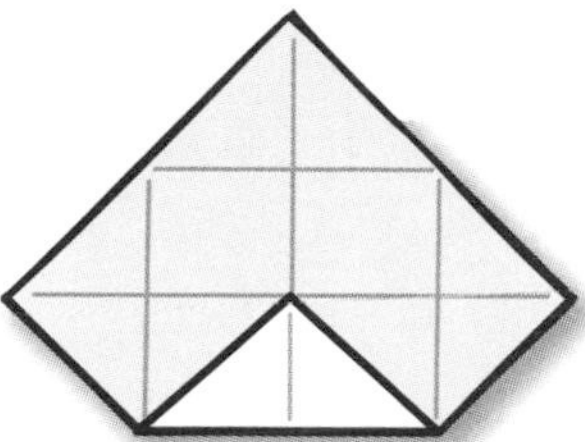

5. Fold the four corners so the points touch at the center of the square. Crease and unfold.

6. Fold one corner so that its point touches the farthest creased line opposite it. Repeat with the other three corners. Then fold the point of each corner to the closest crease line. Crease well and unfold. Look at the pattern of squares on the bottom.

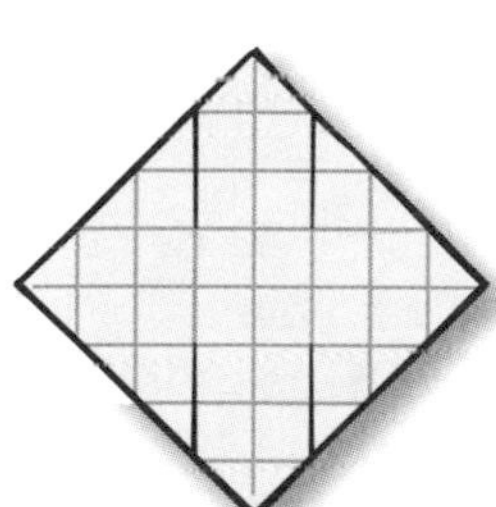

7. Cut lines into the paper at two opposite corners. Cut two squares in and two squares apart.

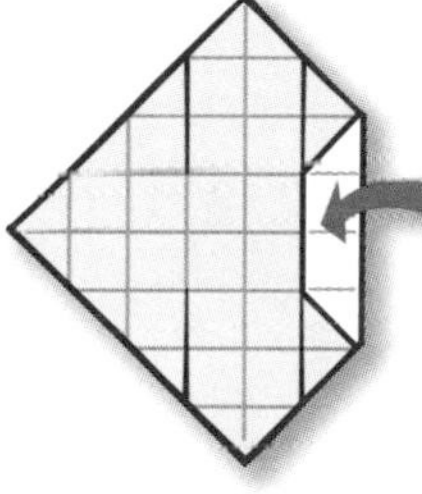

8. Hold the paper in front of you with the cuts at the top and the bottom. Fold in the right and left corners two times along the creased lines, then bend the two sides up.

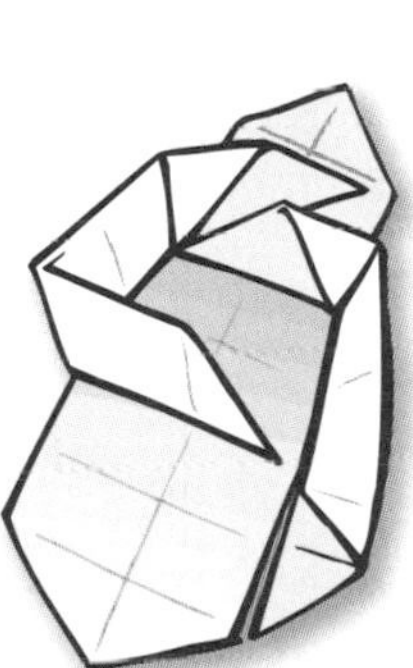

9. Bend the pointed ends toward each other and cross them.

10. Bring the bottom pointed part of the box up over the crossed ends, folding it and tucking it under so it stays put. Do the same for the top pointed part.

11. Optional: Put a drop of glue on the point to make it secure.

12. Follow steps 4 through 10 to make the lid of the box.

Ta Da! You now have a unique box with a lid. How many ways can you think of to use it?

* See page 208 for the metric conversion chart.

Arts and crafts are fun hobbies. You get to be creative and make new treasures for yourself and others.

Activity:

Decoupage a Pencil Holder

Decoupage means decorating with paper cutouts. Originally, decoupage artists cut out paper designs and glued them to furniture. When the furniture was varnished, it looked as if the designs had been painted on.

What You Need

- A clean soup can
- Paint
- Paintbrush
- Glue
- Cup of water
- Paper towels
- Pictures cut out from magazines, postcards, greeting cards, wrapping paper, or photos, or decal stickers
- Decoupage medium or varnish

What You Do

1. Peel the label off the empty can.
2. Paint all around the can and let it dry.
3. Wash the brush; then dry it.
4. Glue pictures on the can.
5. Use the decoupage medium or varnish and coat the entire can. Let it dry.
6. Do a second coat and allow it to dry completely.

You can decoupage family photos onto a can or a box to capture memories! Try using the photos that aren't perfect—the ones where someone's eyes are closed or they have a goofy grin. After getting the okay from your parents, you can cut the photos up and use the good parts.

Activity:

Sponge Prints

You can use lots of things to make interesting prints: leaves coated with paint, vegetables, or pieces of foam. Also, white glue squiggled onto a square of cardboard, allowed to dry, and then pressed into paint can make a print. Try making sponge prints. They're great for greeting cards or wrapping paper.

What You Need

- Wax paper or other nonabsorbent paper
- Scissors
- Piece of sponge
- Water-based paint or ink
- Bowl
- Blank cards or paper

What You Do

1. Cover your work surface with newspapers.
2. Draw your design on the wax paper.
3. Cut out the design. The leftover paper is your "stencil," which is what you will use to make your prints.
4. Pour the paint or ink into the bowl.
5. Dip the sponge into the paint or ink, or use a small brush to put paint or ink onto the sponge.
6. Press the stencil over a card or sheet of paper. Dab the sponge over the stencil to make a print. Be careful not to use too much ink or paint on the sponge. Tap off the excess onto newspaper.

Do More

If you like art activities like decoupage and sponge printing, check out these badges in the *Junior Girl Scout Badge Book:*

Sometimes the process of making art is more interesting than the actual product. Consider the fun you can have making a papier-mâché *piñata* with a group of friends. It might turn out lumpy or lop-sided, but you will get lots of laughs while creating your cow, pig, horse, or whatever other shape you choose.

Safety Tips

When you are ready to break your *piñata,* you need to follow some safety rules:

1. Each person gets only three tries while the rest of the group stands clear.
2. The *piñata* can be raised or lowered on a rope so that it is easier to hit for a particular person.
3. No one is allowed to rush in after the candy until the person who broke the *piñata* has put down the stick and taken her blindfold off.

Activity:

The Perfect Piñata

Although most people think of them as Mexican, the first *piñatas* were actually made in Italy. *Piñatas* used to be made out of clay, but now most are papier-mâché. They are often made into animal shapes, but you can make yours any shape you choose.

After a *piñata* is made and filled with treasures, such as candy and toys, people take turns trying to break it open. Each person is blindfolded and given a stick to bat at the *piñata.* When the *piñata* breaks, the treasures fall to the ground and everyone scrambles to pick them up.

What You Need

- Old newspapers
- Scissors
- Strong balloon
- Masking tape
- Liquid starch (find in the supermarket)
- Aluminum pie plate
- Pin or needle for making holes
- Wrapped candy, small toys, and/or other treasures to put inside
- Paints and paintbrushes
- Art tissue paper
- String

What You Do

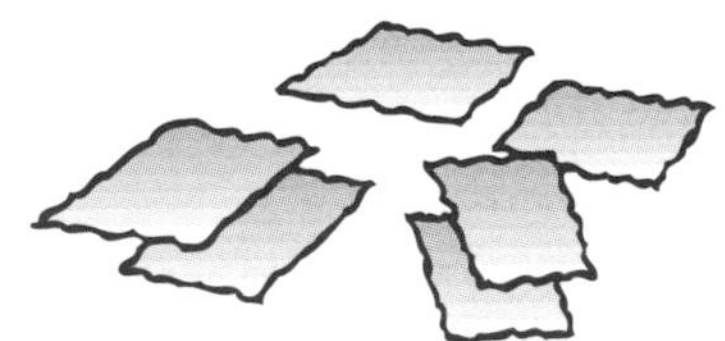

1. Tear or cut the newspapers into small squares about 1 inch* in size.

5. Let the whole thing dry very well. You will probably need to leave it overnight or even for a couple of days.

9. After you've finished filling the *piñata,* cover the hole with several layers of masking tape. Make sure not to cover the holes that you will use to hang it.

2. Blow up the balloon, tie it off, and tape it onto the table.

3. Pour the liquid starch into the pie plate. Dip a square of newspaper in the starch and stick it on the balloon.

4. Repeat until you have covered the balloon with three or four layers of newspaper squares. (Don't cover the tied end of the balloon.)

6. When the *piñata* is dry, remove the balloon by pinching the end and poking the balloon with the pin. Pull the deflated balloon out of its newspaper shell.

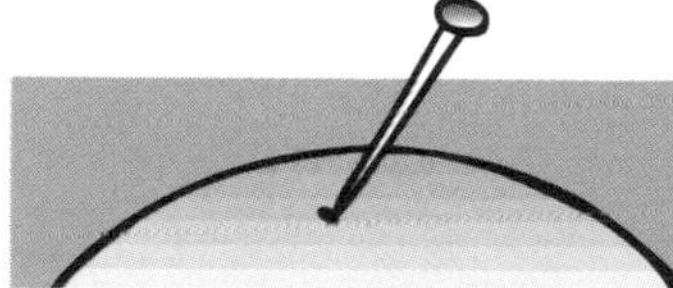

7. With the pin, make two small holes in the *piñata* for use in hanging it up.

8. Fill the *piñata* with whatever prizes you choose.

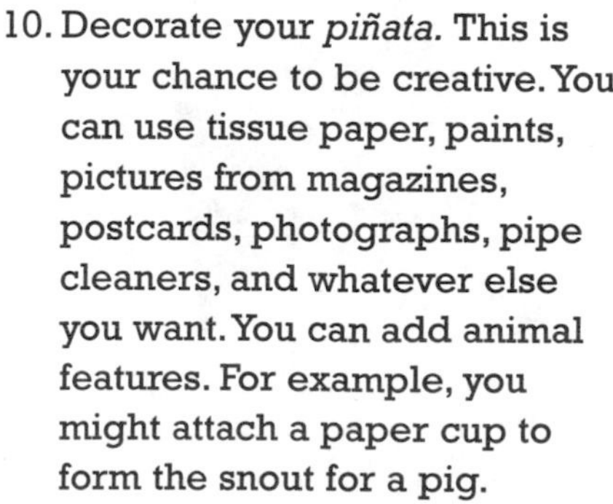

10. Decorate your *piñata.* This is your chance to be creative. You can use tissue paper, paints, pictures from magazines, postcards, photographs, pipe cleaners, and whatever else you want. You can add animal features. For example, you might attach a paper cup to form the snout for a pig.

11. Put the string through the holes so that the *piñata* is ready for hanging.

Read More

Get some party ideas in the "Family and Friends" chapter of this book. Make a *piñata* for your next party.

* See page 208 for the metric conversion chart.

The Wonders of Writing

Reading and writing are two great ways to spend your time because they let you use your imagination. When you are reading, you can lose yourself in the story. You can become one of the story's characters. When you are writing, you can put down on paper your thoughts and feelings, reports about your day, poems, or stories. A good way to do this is by keeping a journal. You can buy one in a store, make one yourself, or use a computer.

You can also express your creativity in writing by:

1. Posting your stories on Web sites and e-zines for other kids to read.
2. Creating your own storybook that you illustrate and write for younger children.
3. Writing letters to friends.
4. Joining the school newspaper staff or literary club.

Disappear into a Book

A good book lets you escape into another world. Reading can transport you to faraway places. Reading can also introduce you to fascinating people and to different ways of life.

Think about all the characters in the books you have read. Which ones did you like the best? Did you like them because they were like you, or because they were NOT like you?

Now make up your own fictional character. Give her a name, a hometown, a best friend. What are her favorite hobbies? Describe her family. What does she want to be when she grows up? What are her strong points? Her weak points? (Maybe she is always late, or she forgets to do things.) Over the next few days, think about how your character would react in certain situations. How would she feel? What would she say? What would she do? After you get to know her, write a story about her.

Activity:

Character for a Day

Host a party where all the guests must dress as their favorite characters from books, plays, or movies. Everyone can guess what characters the others are pretending to be. Afterwards, have each person explain why she chose to be her particular character.

Do More

If you like reading and writing, check out these badges in the *Junior Girl Scout Badge Book.*

Write All About It

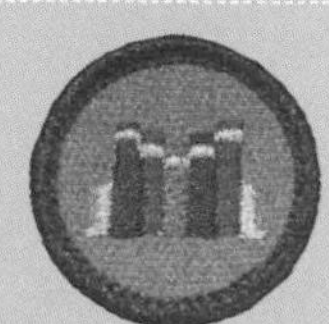
Books

Ms. Fix-It

Becoming handy—working with wood and tools and knowing how to fix things—is not only a useful and inventive skill, but it also saves you money and teaches you skills that may lead to certain careers.

Know Your Tools

These are the basic tools that should be in every home tool kit.

Hammer

For pounding and removing nails. Make sure the hammer is the right weight for you. You should be able to hold it comfortably near the end of the handle. Flip your wrist back, then forward, when you pound.

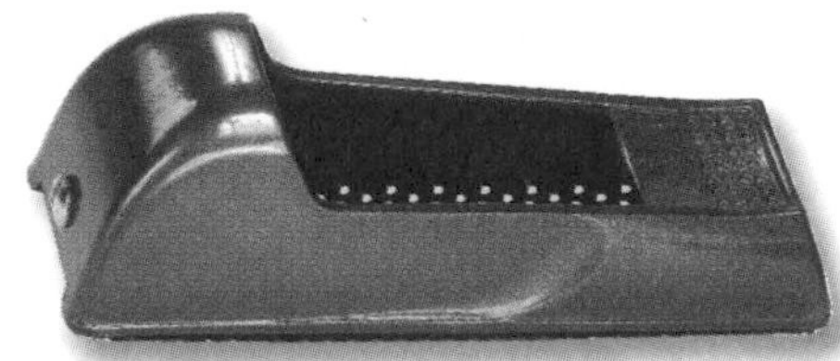

Plane

For making wood smooth or smaller. Use a plane that fits comfortably in your hands. Make sure that your board is in a vise (a tool that grips the wood) to hold it steady. Use both hands and move the plane in one direction only.

Saw

For cutting wood or metal. You will probably use a common saw or cross cut saw for most projects. Use one that is about 16 inches* long or slightly longer, depending on the length of your arm.

Sandpaper

For smoothing rough surfaces. Sandpaper can be wrapped around and tacked to a block of wood to make it steady. Coarse sandpaper should be used for your first sanding. Use finer grains for finishing.

Tips for Tool Safety

- Always make sure that you have completely learned how to use a tool before you start to work with it.
- Never use power tools unless an adult is present who knows how to use them.
- Make sure you have a clear and steady work surface.
- Keep tools out of the reach of younger children.
- Make sure the tools you are using are in good condition.
- Wear goggles to protect your eyes, particularly if you are hammering, sawing, or drilling.

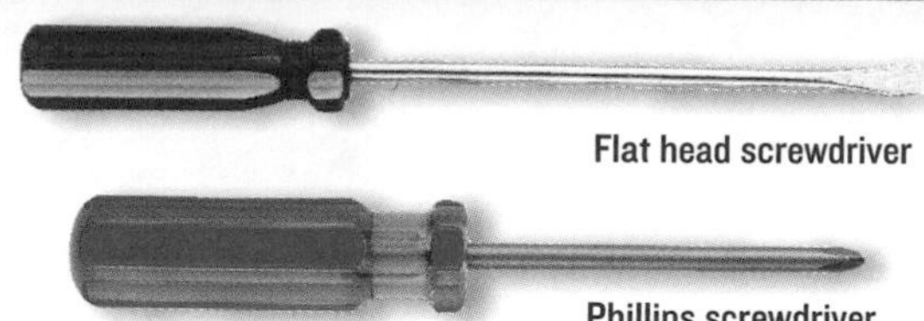
Flat head screwdriver
Phillips screwdriver

Screwdriver

For turning screws. In the illustration, you can see two types of screwdrivers. Each type works with a particular type of screw. The tip of the Phillips screwdriver has a cross shape. The straight screwdriver has one flat line.

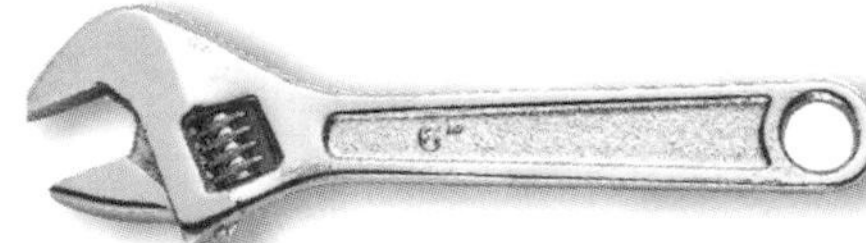

Wrench

For turning nuts and bolts.

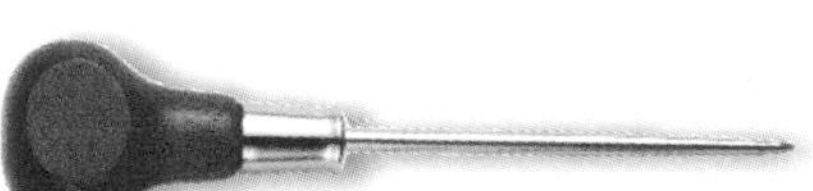

Awl

For making holes. An awl helps you mark where you want to put a nail. It can also start the hole for a screw.

Level

For keeping angles and edges straight.

Drill

For making deep holes. Drills must be used with care. Make sure you read Tips for Tool Safety before using one.

Pliers

For gripping things. Pliers can help you make things tight or loosen things that are stuck.

Use Your Tools

After you've put together a home tool kit, these projects will help you practice using them:

- Use a level and a hammer to hang a picture.
- Use sandpaper to fix a door or window that sticks.
- Use a screwdriver or wrench to tighten screws or bolts that have become loose.
- Use a wrench to replace a washer in a leaky faucet.

Doing Repairs

Find someone to show you how to do some of these home repairs:

- Fix a hole in a window screen.
- Fix a loose chair or table leg.
- Install batteries in a flashlight or smoke detector.
- Caulk around a bathtub, shower, window, or door.
- Unclog a sink, bathtub, or toilet.
- Repair a crack in a wall.
- Repair broken pottery.

* See page 208 for the metric conversion chart.

Make a Catch Board

This board can be used to hang keys, memo pads, eyeglasses, or jewelry.

What You Need

- A flat, wooden board
- At least 12 nails (each about 2 inches* long)
- Hammer
- Medium-grain sandpaper
- Small block of wood (about the size of a bar of soap)
- Paintbrush
- Pliers
- A rag
- Heavy cord or string
- Saw
- Paint or clear varnish
- Drill (or two ring-topped screws)

What You Do

1. Saw the board to measure 12 inches by 18 inches.*
2. Wrap the sandpaper around the small wood block, and smooth the edges and surface of the board.
3. Rub the board with a rag to remove any dust.
4. Paint or varnish the board. You can paint designs, paste on pictures, drawings, or decorative pieces of paper and then coat with a clear varnish, or draw with a permanent ink marker and then coat with a clear varnish.
5. Let your decorated board dry for at least 24 hours.
6. Hammer nails 1/2 inch* to 1 inch* deep in various places on the board. Whatever you want to keep on the board will hang from these nails.
7. Grip the nail heads with the pliers and bend each nail upward to make a hook.
8. You can prepare the board for hanging in two different ways. Use method A if you have a drill for making holes; use method B if you do not.
   A. Drill holes in the top corners of the board.
   B. You will need two ring-topped screws for this hanging method. These screws will go on the top corners of the board. Start holes for the screws by using an awl or by gently hammering nails into the spots for the screws. Pull the nails out and put the screws into place. Turn them until they fit tightly. If turning becomes difficult, insert a screwdriver through the ring opening and turn.
9. Thread the cord through the holes (or rings) and then knot the ends so that the cord will not pull through.

Do More

If you like fix-it projects and repair work, check out the Ms. Fix-It badge in the *Junior Girl Scout Badge Book.*

Ms. Fix-It

* See page 208 for the metric conversion chart.

I'm a Tekkie Girl and Proud of It

Technology is the application of science. It is using what people have learned about how the world works to create practical things that help people live. For example, a bird can fluff its feathers to create air pockets, which insulate the bird from the cold. So the warm, lightweight jacket you wear may use material that imitates bird feathers, or it can be made out of the real thing—down!

Activity:

Share a Hobby

Discover a recreational activity that uses technology. Share the activity or knowledge of the activity with your group. For example, display photos or a videotape you have taken; sing karaoke; direct the movements of a model car, boat, or plane you have built; bake bread using a breadmaker; sew something on a sewing machine; use exercise equipment with the help of an adult; or display something you have made using a computer graphics program. Explain how technology is used to make your activity more fun or to save time.

Test Yourself: *Find the Inventions*

Technology is a lot more than computers! You probably don't even think about how much you use technology every day. How many examples of technology can you find in the following story?

Christina woke up to the music from her clock radio and tumbled out of bed. She headed for the bathroom, where she brushed her teeth with her electric toothbrush, and then took a warm shower. After drying off with a thick towel, she looked into her mirror—she was lucky it was the kind guaranteed not to fog in a steamy bathroom—and used a blow-dryer on her hair. Then she added some curl to her bangs with her curling iron.

Christina put on her new bike shorts that were guaranteed to keep her dry and slipped on her Girl Scout T-shirt. She went to the kitchen, where she popped a piece of bread into the toaster and zapped hot water in the microwave for her cocoa. While she was waiting for her socks to dry in the dryer, she checked her e-mail on the kitchen computer, and looked for the weather report on the Internet. "Perfect," she said to herself. It was going to be sunny all day, so she knew her bike trip was still on.

She picked up a pen and wrote a Post-It™ note to her mom, who had already left to return last night's videocassette and to do other errands in the car. Christina stuck her note on the refrigerator. She poured her cocoa into a thermal cup with a lid, slathered peanut butter on her toast, and headed out the door with her fanny pack, which her mom had helped her pack the night before. She was looking forward to eating the energy bars that she knew were inside. Christina wheeled her mountain bike out of the garage, put on her bike helmet, and joined her friend Samantha who was waiting for her in the driveway.

How did you do?

You probably knew that examples of technology included the clock radio, electric toothbrush, fogless mirror, blow-dryer, curling iron, toaster, microwave, dryer, computer, bicycle, videocassette, car, thermal cup, and bike helmet. But did you also pick out these?

- Bathroom and shower
- Towel
- Bike shorts
- Bread
- Pen
- Post-It™ notes
- Peanut butter
- Fanny pack
- Energy bars

Technology is used to create the food we eat, the clothes we wear, and many other products we use every day.

9 Explore and Discover

In This Chapter You Will Learn About:

"I'm going on my first camping trip . . . what's the weather going to be like?"

"My eyes are stinging. Is there too much chlorine in the pool?"

"I promised to bring these cookies to our fundraiser but the recipe calls for baking powder and there's none in the house. What can I substitute?"

"My philodendron looks droopy. What can I do to make it healthy?"

The exploring you do in everyday life, and in this chapter, could lead you to new hobbies or interests, as well as a deeper understanding of how and why things happen.

Check out the activities in the next few pages. There is no limit to the fun things you can find out if you let yourself explore!

Activity:

Be a Detective

Here are some examples of questions you can ask to help you explore and discover new things:

Observing things: What does it look like? How does it sound? What does it feel like? How does it move?

Comparing things: How are they alike? How are they different?

Imagining and creating: What if. . . ? What do I think will happen? How can I solve this problem? How can I change this to make it do something different?

Making a hypothesis: A hypothesis is a guess that you make based on what you observe and the information you collect. Then you try to find out if your guess is right. "Why does it do this?" "If it does this, then what is likely to happen?" "How can I be sure that. . . ?" "How can I find out?"

Activity:

The Incredible Slurping Plant

Sometimes the most fun discoveries are those you make with simple objects at home. Here's a great invention that uses common household items to create a watering system for a plant. It's especially great for people who forget to water!

What You Need

- A 2-pint* plastic container with a lid
- Potted plant (Start with a 6- to 8-inch* diameter pot)
- Scissors
- Pen with a point
- Cotton string
- Newspaper for your table
- Water

What You Do

1. With the lid on, use the pen to poke a hole in the middle of your plastic container lid so that the string can pass through easily.

2. Fill the container with water and soak about 18 inches* of string in the water.

3. Gently remove the plant from its pot and set aside.

4. Take the string out of the water and coil it in loops on the bottom of the empty plant pot. Run one end of the string through a hole in the middle of the pot's bottom so that it hangs down at least 8 inches*.

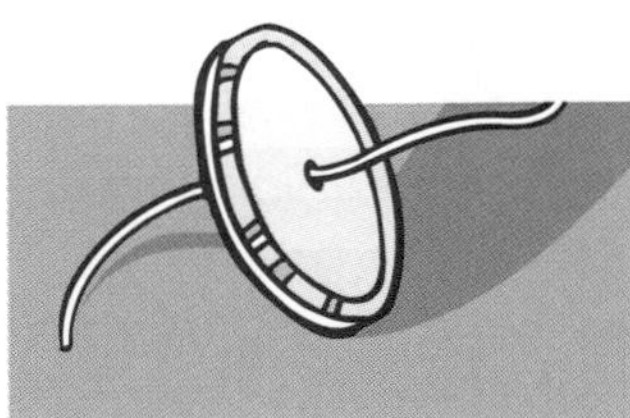

5. Thread the hanging string through the top of the plastic lid. Make sure that the string is not stuck to the underside of the lid. Fit the lid back onto the container with water. The string will eventually drop to the bottom.

6. Place your plant back into the pot, which should be resting on the lid. If the soil around the plant is not moist, water it from the top once, just enough to dampen it.

7. Voilà! Set your plant in a place that gets light. You might even want to set it in a basket.

You shouldn't have to water your plant from the top any more. Check the water level in the container and add water by raising the lid carefully on one side. Use a water bottle or watering can with a spout to pour water into the container. You might want to clean the container once a month, adding fresh water.

* See page 208 for the metric conversion chart.

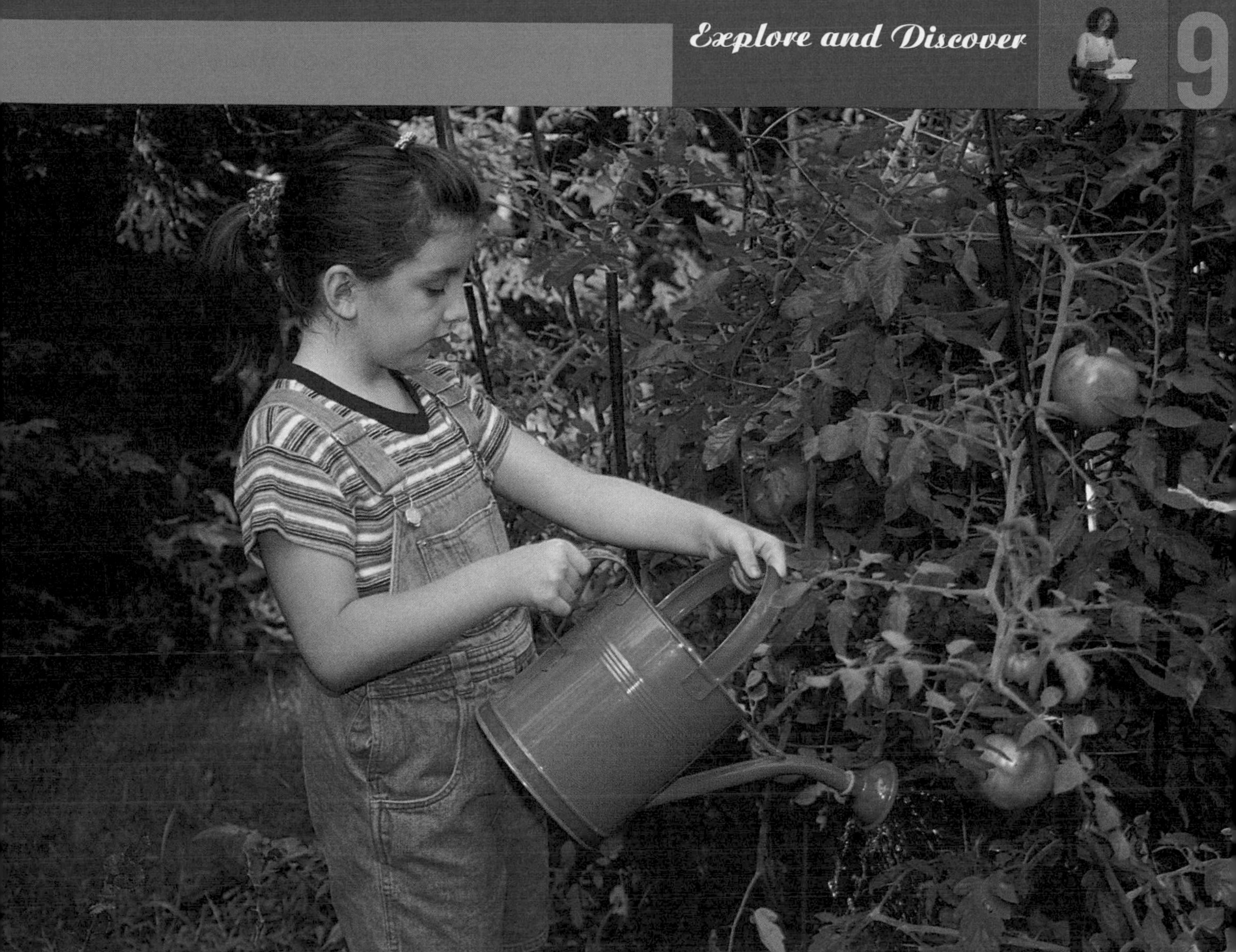

Why Does This Happen?

The movement of the water up the string is called capillary action. You might recognize the word capillary as a word that refers to tiny blood vessels in the body. Capillary actually means any long, thin tube. All plants have capillaries (even tall trees). The string has spaces that form tubes as well. Sponges absorb water by capillary action, as do many kinds of natural fibers used for clothing. (What happens if you walk through puddles wearing jeans?)

Do More

For more fun activities with water movement, check out Girls Ask Why on the "Just for Girls" page of the Girl Scouts Web site *www.girlscouts.org*.

Kitchen Chemist

Scientists group chemicals that have common properties. pH describes how acid or how alkaline (base) a substance is. The pH of a substance is measured by a special scale developed by scientists. The scale runs from 0 to 14, with the middle being 7 (or neutral), 0 being the most acid, and 14 the most alkaline.

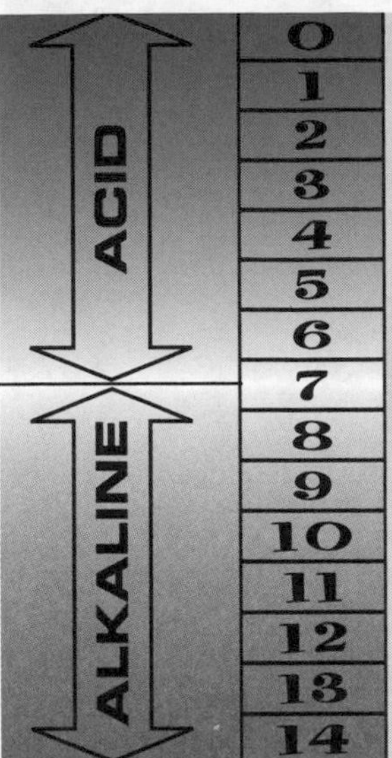

pH	Substance
0	
1	Stomach juices
2	Battery acid
3	Apple juice, soft drink
4	Tomato juice
5	Black coffee
6	Normal rain water
7	Pure water—NEUTRAL
8	Human blood
9	Seawater
10	Milk of magnesia
11	Household ammonia
12	Baking soda
13	Lye
14	

Some foods contain acids, like lemon juice and vinegar. They taste sour. Bases have no strong taste in foods, and often feel slippery or soapy to the touch. Liquid bleach is a base. (Many acids and bases are poisonous, so don't assume you can taste them to find out their pH!)

Water and soil are tested for their pH for a lot of reasons. If a swimming pool is too acid, it will burn your eyes. That's why you see the lifeguard testing the water on a regular basis. If a pond is too acid, the fish will die. Something acid can be made less so by adding a base.

People who garden, raise fish, or have a home pool, often act as chemists when they test and change the pH of the soil or water by adding an acid or base. Doctors, soil scientists, atmospheric scientists, and fish biologists often ask questions about pH as part of their daily work.

Laws have been passed in our country to lessen the amount of polluting chemicals from factories and automobiles that combine with water in the air to create harmful acid rain, which is a problem worldwide.

To test for pH, you can buy a specially treated paper, called litmus paper (narrow range), from a drugstore. Follow the directions on the package to test substances.

Do More

If you like the activities you've been doing so far in this chapter, check out these badges in the *Junior Girl Scout Badge Book:*

Science in Everyday Life

Earth Connections

Plants and Animals

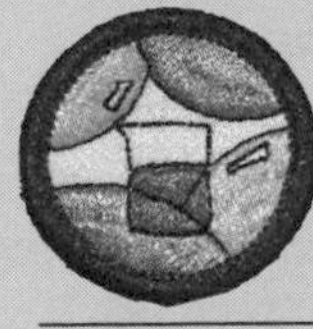

Science Discovery

Science Sleuth

Activity:

Investigate and Broadcast

Find a woman in your community who works in the fields of math, science, or technology. Interview her about her career. Here are some questions you could ask:

- How did she get interested in her career?
- What specific questions has she asked, and what answers has she found?
- Did she, or does she, face difficulties because she is a woman?
- How is her work contributing to science and technology today?

After you have finished the interview, you can do any or all of the following:

1. Write a story about the woman and share it on the "Just for Girls" Web site, under Thought-Catchers.

2. Have a "story exchange" with friends who have interviewed other women about their careers.

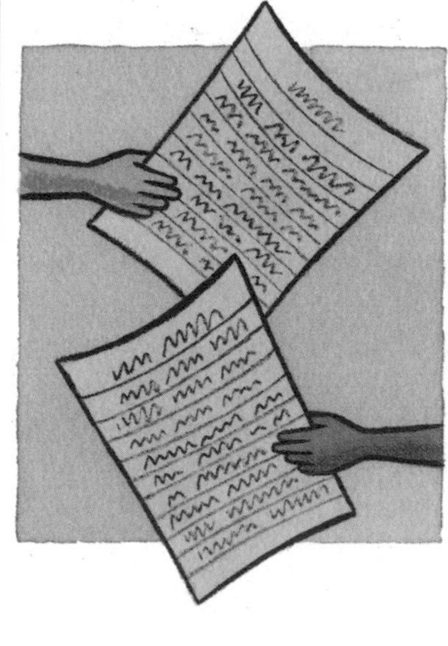

3. Create a display during Women's History Month (March) or during one of the weeks that celebrate science and technology throughout the year. (See the Science section of the "Just for Girls" Event Calendar on the Web site.)

Mix It Up as a Cook

Did you know that you use math skills and scientific principles when you cook? If you measure the wrong amounts of ingredients, your cookies could taste terrible. If you don't let your bread dough rise, your bread will be too tough. Cooking can be a wonderful hobby. It's creative and relaxing and you and your friends can enjoy the end results of your hobby.

Do More

If the kitchen is your favorite room in the house, or if you just like to make tasty treats, you might want to try these badges in the *Junior Girl Scout Badge Book:*

Let's Get Cooking

Outdoor Cook

Activity:

Twist and Shape

Pretzels are easy and fun to make for a party. You can invite friends over for a bake-off. And you don't have to make traditional-looking pretzels; once you have made the dough, you can create whatever shapes you choose. Here's how:

What You Need

- 1 package of yeast
- 1-1/2 cups* lukewarm water
- 3/4 teaspoon* salt
- 1-1/2 teaspoons* sugar
- 4 cups* flour
- 1 egg
- Coarse salt
- Pastry brush or clean paintbrush

What You Do

1. In a large bowl, soften the yeast in the water.

2. Add the sugar and salt to the water mixture.

3. Little by little, add in the flour.

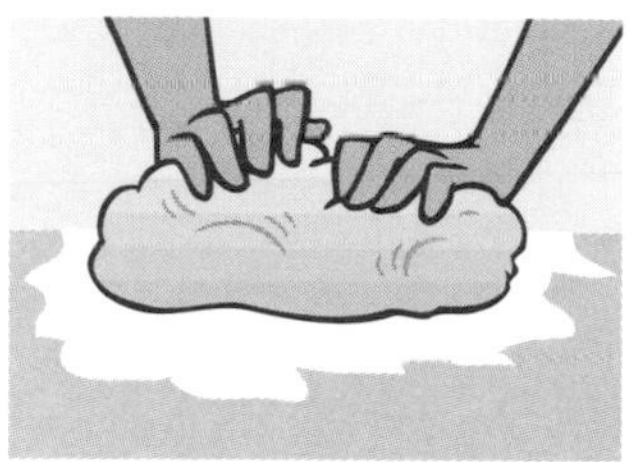

4. Once all the flour is added, use your hands (make sure you wash them first) to knead the mixture into a smooth, soft dough.

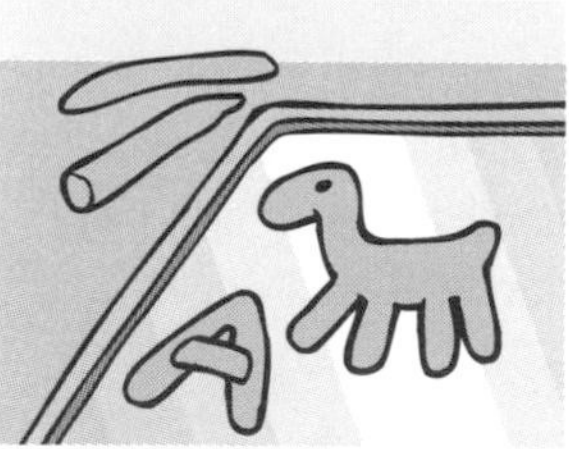

5. Cut the dough into small chunks and begin sculpting. You can turn the dough into anything from alphabet letters to zoo animals. Work on top of a lightly greased cookie tray so that you won't have to move your creations when you are ready to bake them.

6. Using a fork, beat the egg in a small bowl. Brush a small amount of egg onto each of the "pretzels" that you have made (this will help them to turn golden brown as they cook). You can also sprinkle a small amount of coarse salt on the pretzels if you choose, or cinnamon sugar.

7. Bake the pretzels at 425 degrees* for 15 minutes, or until golden brown.

8. EAT!

Do More

See the "Be Healthy, Be Fit" chapter for some healthy recipes.

* See page 208 for the metric conversion chart.

How Computer-wise Are You?

Our life is becoming more and more dependent on computer technology. It only makes sense to be informed so you can keep up and take advantage of everything this wonderful world has to offer.

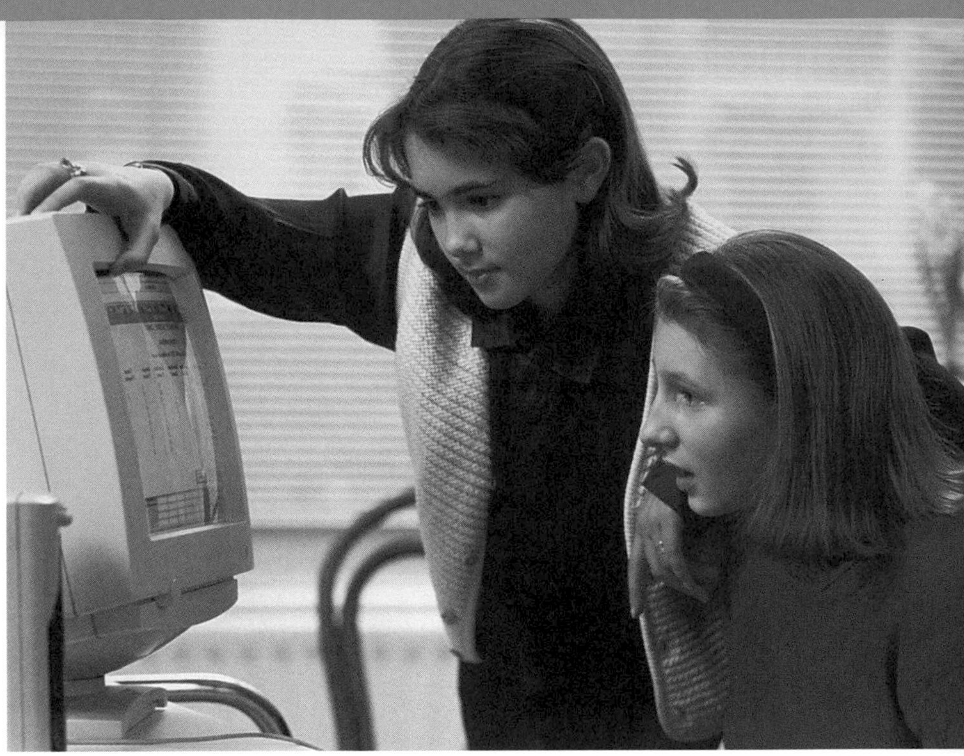

NEED HELP WITH THE LINGO?

If computer words are tripping you up, this list of definitions should help.

Bookmark: A method of saving your favorite pages that you find on the Internet so that you can return to them easily.

Safety Pledge: A pledge to act safely while on the Internet, found on many kids' sites, including *www.girlscouts.org*.

Chat: A method of communicating to other people on the Internet at a specific address. Usually done in a "chat room."

Link: A specific Web site address, which, when entered into your Internet browser or clicked on within a page, takes you to a page on the Internet or a place on that Web page.

E-mail: Written messages that are sent via electronic signal through telephone lines or wireless satellite transmission.

Search engine: A database made up of Web files, that allows you to find something specific on the Internet.

Web site: An address on the World Wide Web that contains pictures and information. A Web site can have many Web pages.

If you don't have a computer or a connection to the Internet, you can find many places to get online. Ask your parents, Girl Scout leader, or a teacher to help you check these out:

- Science museum
- School
- Library
- Workplace
- Friend's house
- Computer store training center
- Girl Scout council

Before you begin, make sure you read the Safety Pledge on "Just for Girls" *www.girlscouts.org*. Or read the section about online safety in the "How to Stay Safe" chapter of this book.

Computer Fun and Games

Do you want to see things from a different perspective? Do you want to experience things that you might never do in real life? Or do you simply want to feel more organized about your regular life? Then saddle up, cyberspace cowgirl, because it's time to find a computer software program that's right for you!

The first step is to figure out what you want to do. Check out these ideas:

- Create a family tree or genealogy chart
- Create a favorite recipe file
- Create a plan for a garden
- Keep a weekly budget for a month
- Index the family holiday card addressees
- Keep track of a collection
- Enhance a special interest or hobby
- Make a plan for a room rearrangement

After you decide what you would like to use a computer program for, read software reviews in computer magazines, talk to sales people at a computer store, and check out recommendations from friends and family. You can also find some great links to other sites and software reviews on the "Just for Girls" Web site.

There is almost no limit to what you can do once you have access to cyberspace!

Do More

If you love computers and technology, check out these badges in the *Junior Girl Scout Badge Book:*

Computer Fun

Discovering Technology

Also, check out the CyberGirlScout badge on the "Just for Girls" section of the Girl Scout Web site.

Test Yourself: *Are You Computer Literate?*

"Computer literate" means you know something about computers. Take this quiz and find out where you stand. Give yourself five points for each "Yes, definitely," two points for each "Yes, sort of," and 0 for each "No way" or "What's that?" Now add up your score. How many points did you get?

Fill in the number of points:

☐ 1. I can use a word processing program to do a school assignment.

☐ 2. I can save and print something.

☐ 3. I can alphabetize a list on the computer.

☐ 4. I can use spell-check.

☐ 5. I have used software or the Internet to learn about something.

☐ 6. I have signed an Internet Safety Pledge.(See Chapter 5 for more information.)

☐ 7. I have sent e-mail to or posted a story or question on the Girl Scouts' "Just for Girls" Web site www.girlscouts.org.

☐ 8. I can use a search engine on the Internet to find out about something I am interested in.

☐ 9. I can bookmark my favorite links.

☐ 10. I can send e-mail to a relative or friend.

☐ 11. I have participated in a computer chat room.

☐ 12. I have used clip-art or a desktop publishing program to create something.

☐ 13. I have helped to build a Web page.

☐ 14. I have visited a computer store or checked out a computer magazine.

☐ 15. I know the best way to sit in relation to my computer keyboard and screen so that I don't do damage to my body or eyes.

☐ **Total points**

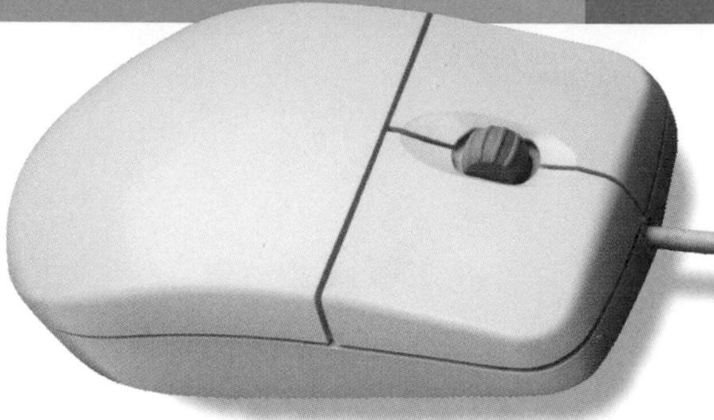

MY Online Safety Pledge

I will not give out personal information such as my address, telephone number, parents' or guardian's work address/telephone number, or the name and location of my school without the permission of my parents or guardian.

I will tell an adult right away if I come across any information that makes me feel uncomfortable.

I will never agree to get together with someone I "meet" online without first checking with my parents or guardian. If my parents or guardian agree to the meeting, I will arrange it in a public place and bring a parent or guardian along.

I will never send a person my picture or anything else without first checking with my parents or guardian.

I will not respond to any messages that are mean or that in any way make me uncomfortable. It is not my fault if I get a message like that. If I do, I will tell my parents or guardian right away so that they can contact the online service.

I will talk with my parents or guardian so that we can set up rules for going online. We will decide on the time of day that I can be online, the length of time I can be online, and appropriate areas for me to visit. I will not access other areas or break these rules without their permission.

Now add up your score. How many points did you get?

0-25
Get moving on the technology highway!

26-45
"Log on" and upgrade your skills!

46-64
Way to go girl! You know your way.

65-75
Hey cybergirl! How about teaching others what you know?

Stayed Tuned Up

Although computers and other technology are an important part of life today, too much of anything is not good for the mind or the body. Here are some guidelines that all kids should be aware of:

1. **Develop your brain.** Don't depend on technology to entertain you all the time. Read a book, get outdoors, talk face to face with people. Build your own life experiences rather than depending upon TV or a computer game that doesn't really help you navigate the real world. Couch potatoes, game-girls, and people who hang out in chat rooms all the time sometimes lose touch with reality. Remember: the computer cannot think for you. It's only a tool to help you. And don't forget to use your judgment. Just because you find something on the Internet or print it out on paper doesn't mean that it is true!

2. **Protect your eyes.** Don't sit too close to the computer or the TV. Make sure you aren't looking at a reflection in the screen. What can you do to protect yourself?

- Use soothing color combinations on the computer screen
- Make sure your screen is bright enough to see the text clearly.
- Remember: computers aren't the only things that can hurt your eyes. Wear safety glasses when recommended for science and sports activities.

Eye doctors recommend that time at the computer be limited to no more than two hours each day for growing kids and teens.

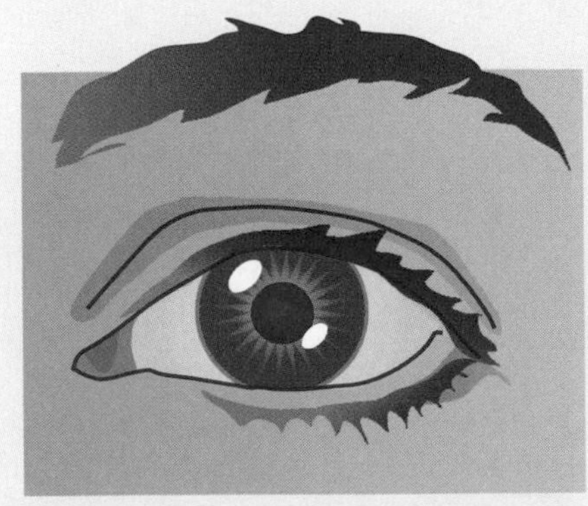

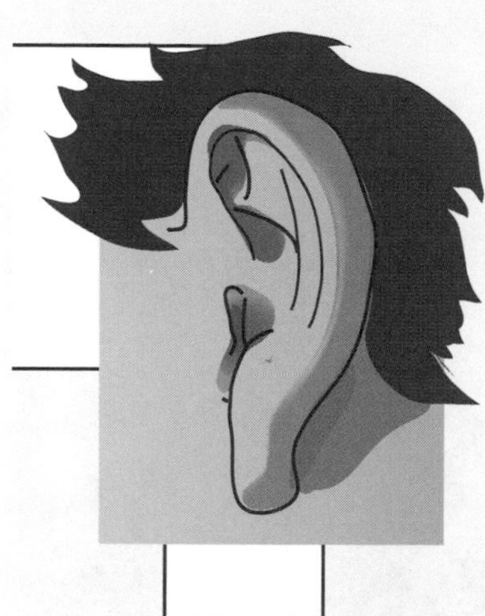

3. Protect your ears. Keep the volume down on earphones and speakers to preserve your hearing (and the hearing of those around you). Use ear protectors when working with loud machinery, like a lawn mower or a sander in a wood shop.

4. Be good to your body. Your muscles and bones are still forming, and mistreating them now could lead to serious problems when you are an adult. Repetitious movements, like using a computer keyboard, can put strain on your muscles and tendons. Take frequent breaks and don't sit or stand in one position for long periods of time. Make sure that you have a chair that adjusts or is the right height for you when using a computer and that your body is in the neutral and relaxed position shown in the illustration.

- Head and neck balanced, with computer monitor even with your eyes
- Your back supported by the chair
- Your shoulders and arms at ease
- Hands and wrists straight out, not up or down
- Feet resting on a foot rest, with knees open

You might need to work with adults to adjust a computer station to your needs. It helps to use an adjustable keyboard, a footrest, an adjustable mouse holder, a pillow for your back if the chair is too big, and a monitor riser for the computer screen.

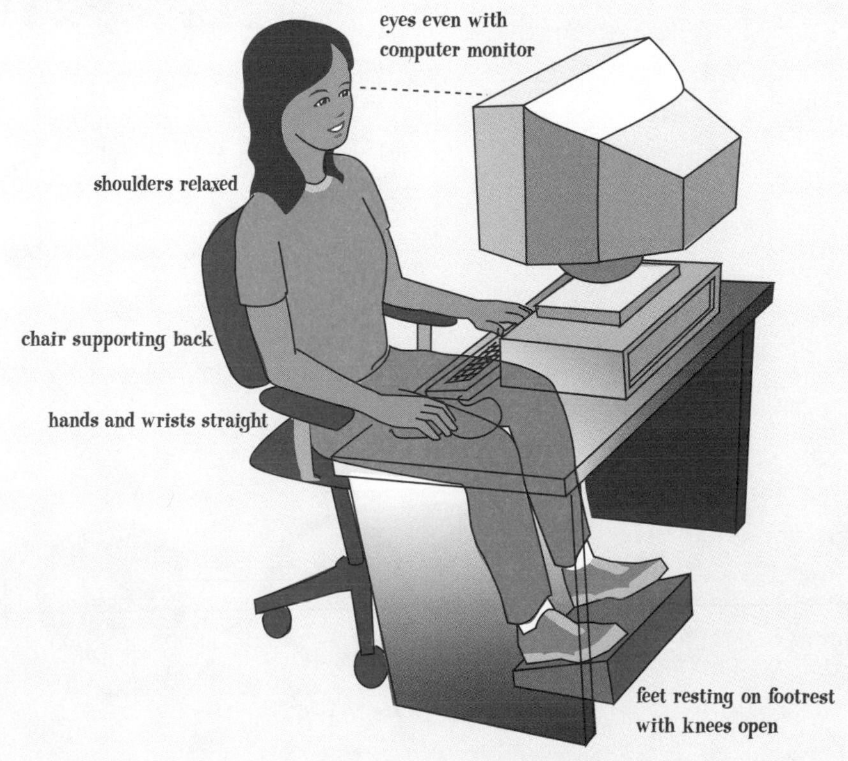

Making Music

Do you and your friends love music? Most people do, even if they can't sing a note or play an instrument. If you love to listen to music, you might try to make it even more part of your life. Here are some ideas.

1. **Learn to play an instrument.** This can become a hobby that you enjoy throughout your life. Maybe you are lucky enough to be able to take lessons at school. If you don't want to take formal lessons, you can buy a teach-yourself-to-play book, video, or computer program.

2. **Sing.** You could sing in a choir, a school glee club, around a campfire, or in the shower!

3. **Produce your own music.** This gives you a chance to pretend you are a disc jockey, record producer, or radio announcer. See the activity box on the next page to find out how.

4. **Write your own song lyrics.** Pick a tune you like, or make up one of your own, and write words to fit the tune. Pick a theme for your song: a season, love, friendship, a story. Listen to some music you like and pay attention to the words. Does the songwriter use rhyming words or lots of one-syllable or multi-syllable words? How do the lyrics fit the melody?

Do More

If making music is for you, try these badges from the *Junior Girl Scout Badge Book:*

Making Music

Music Fan

Activity:

Be a Disc Jockey

What You Need

- A way to record music, such as a tape and tape recorder
- Favorite friends with favorite songs

What You Do

1. Decide what the theme of your music party will be. Do you want to highlight a certain artist? A certain kind of music? Or a theme, such as songs about places around the world? Do you want your new tape to have only songs you would like to hear on a rainy Monday morning or ones that would make everyone get up and dance?
2. Ask each of your friends to give you songs on either a CD or a cassette that fit the theme you have chosen.
3. Decide the order that the music should be played. Do you want to have slow songs mixed with fast ones? Do you want classic rock combined with hip-hop? After you have decided on the order, record your new tape and invite all your friends over to enjoy it!

10 Junior Girl Scout Awards

By doing certain activities, Junior Girl Scouts can earn not only badges, but other awards. When you wear these awards on your sash or vest, everyone can see what you have achieved as a Junior Girl Scout! In this chapter you will find out about specific awards that you can earn.

In This Chapter You Will Learn About:

Junior Girl Scout Badges

"Badges," as Juliette Gordon Low said, "show that you have done something so often and so well that you can teach it to someone else." The *Junior Girl Scout Badge Book* contains all the badges that you are eligible to earn as a Junior Girl Scout. There are over 100 badges, covering a number of different topics. You can pick topics that you are already interested in—or try something completely new. You can choose badges to do on your own, with another Girl Scout, or in a group.

Signs

Besides badges, Junior Girl Scouts can earn these four signs: the Sign of the Star, the Sign of the Rainbow, the Sign of the Sun, and the Sign of the World. These four signs, which only Junior Girl Scouts can earn, are based on the four program goals of Girl Scouting. The four program goals describe how you will grow and develop by doing Girl Scout activities.

Sign of the Star

Sign of the Rainbow

Sign of the Sun

Sign of the World

The first program goal is for you to become the very best person you can. You should feel good about yourself and what you have already done, be open to new activities and challenges, and use your talents and skills in new ways. The Sign of the Star is about becoming your best.

The second program goal is for you to learn to respect other people, build strong friendships, and to learn to understand and appreciate people who are different from you. The Sign of the Rainbow is about building relationships.

The third program goal is for you to build your own set of values. These values will help you make decisions and guide your actions. The Sign of the Sun is about values.

The fourth program goal is designed to help you build leadership skills and to contribute to society by helping other people. The Sign of the World is about making your world a better place.

The Junior Aide Award

You can earn the Junior Aide Award when you learn to help with Daisy Girl Scouts or Brownie Girl Scouts. By helping younger girls, you take on a leadership role and become someone for them to look up to.

The Junior Girl Scout Leadership Award

To earn this pin, you do activities that concentrate on building leadership skills. Each step you take toward earning the pin will help you become a better leader.

Bridge to Cadette Girl Scouts Award

During your last year as a Junior Girl Scout, you can begin to do the activities to bridge to Cadette Girl Scouts. You get to do a Cadette Girl Scout activity on the way to earning this award.

The Girl Scout Bronze Award

This is the highest award a Junior Girl Scout can earn! To earn this award, you will do a project that shows that you understand and live by the Girl Scout Promise and Law.

The Sign of the Star

Juliette Low spoke about "little stars that guide us." You can be your own "star" by improving your skills and talents, feeling good about what you have achieved in your life and in Girl Scouts so far, and opening your heart and mind to new activities and experiences. You have the potential to shine brightly as you develop confidence, skills, and talents in your own unique way. In the Sign of the Star, you will do activities that allow you to develop your potential. Here are the requirements:

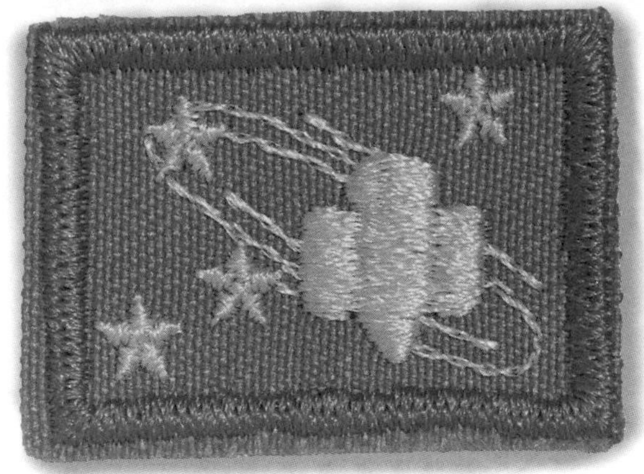

1

Try something new. Earn a badge in a topic that you know nothing about or that teaches you a brand new skill.

Signature:

What I did:

What I learned:

2

Boost your self-esteem (how you feel about yourself). Do at least four activities from the following badges: "A Healthier You," "Being My Best," "Looking Your Best."

Signature:

What I did:

What I learned:

3

Show off your talents. Display or demonstrate one of your talents to your troop, group, or others.

Signature:

What I did:

What I learned:

4

Complete two activities from the "It's Great to Be a Girl" chapter in this book.

Signature:

What I did:

What I learned:

5

Complete an activity from one of the following resources: *GirlSports, Issues for Girl Scouts: Girls Are Great for Junior Girl Scouts*, or the "Just For Girls" section of Girl Scouts of the USA Web site *www.girlscouts.org/girls*. Or participate in a council event.

Signature:

What I did:

What I learned:

The Sign of the Rainbow

The world is made up of a rainbow of people. People are different, yet in many ways they are the same. They share many of the same goals and dreams. In Girl Scouting, you learn to respect the differences in people. You also cooperate with others and work together. In the Sign of the Rainbow, you will do activities that will help you to relate to others with understanding and respect. Here are the requirements:

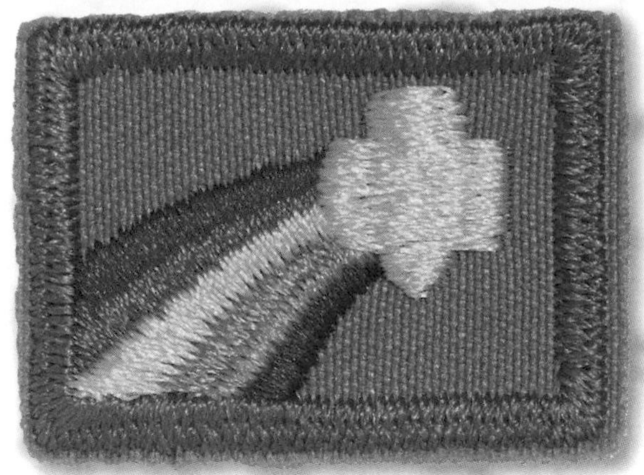

1

Complete one of the following badges to learn more about the people in the world: "World Neighbors," "Global Awareness," "Humans and Habitats."

Signature:

What I did:

What I learned:

2

Do an activity from either *Issues for Girl Scouts: Connections for Junior Girl Scouts,* or *Girl Scouts Go Global.* Or you can participate in a council event in which you get to meet new girls. Be sure to try to make some new friends.

Signature:

What I did:

What I learned:

3

Do an activity from the "Family and Friends" chapter of this book.

Signature:

What I did:

What I learned:

4

Do an activity in which you help others get something done or help them learn a new skill. By helping out where you are needed, you show respect for others.

Signature:

What I did:

What I learned:

5

Do two activities from any of the following badges to learn more about people in your community: "My Community," "Celebrating People," "Local Lore."

Signature:

What I did:

What I learned:

The Sign of the Sun

When you follow your values in your life—remember, values are the things that are most important to you—you have a better sense of where you want to go and how to get there. In the Sign of the Sun, you will do activities that allow you to reflect on and practice both Girl Scout values and personal values. Here are the requirements:

1

Live the Girl Scout Promise. Do an activity in which you serve God, your country, or other people.

Signature:

What I did:

What I learned:

2

Live the Girl Scout Law. Choose one part of the Girl Scout Law and do an activity that helps you to practice it.

Signature:

What I did:

What I learned:

3

Earn one of these badges: "It's Important to Me," "The Choice Is Yours," or "High on Life." Or you can earn the religious recognition of your choice.

Signature:

What I did:

What I learned:

4

Do an activity from "Girl Scout Basics" or "Adventures in Girl Scouting" in this book.

Signature:

What I did:

What I learned:

5

Read the section on values in the "It's Great to Be a Girl" chapter in this book. Read about "Values in Girl Scouting" and answer the "Test Yourself" questions on that page.

Signature:

What I did:

What I learned:

The Sign of the World

Girl Scouts promise to improve the world around them. You build leadership skills and contribute to your society when you do a service project that helps others. The Sign of the World helps you join forces with other Girl Scouts to make a difference in your communities. Here are the requirements:

1

Get started. Read the section on doing a service project in the "Adventures in Girl Scouts" chapter. In a group, discuss some projects that you think your community needs.	**Signature:**
What I did:	
What I learned:	

2

Practice your citizenship skills. Complete one of the following badges: "Model Citizen," or "Lead On."	**Signature:**
What I did:	
What I learned:	

3

Learn more about protecting the world around you. Do an activity from one of the following badges: "Earth Connections," "Eco-Action," or "Your Outdoor Surroundings."

Signature:

What I did:

What I learned:

4

Try an activity from one of the following Girl Scout resources: *Fun and Easy Nature and Science Investigations* or *Issues for Girls Scouts: Read to Lead for Junior Girl Scouts* or *Issues for Girls Scouts: Media Know-How for Junior Girl Scouts* or *Junior Girl Scouts Against Smoking.* Or participate in a council project that helps make the world a better place.

Signature:

What I did:

What I learned:

5

Look at the "Create and Invent" and "Explore and Discover" chapters of this book to find a way to make or do something to improve your neighborhood or community. Now do it!

Signature:

What I did:

What I learned:

The Junior Aide Award

Would you like to learn more about being a leader? Do you enjoy sharing what you know with younger girls? Would you like to test your skills? While earning the Junior Aide award, you will help Daisy, Brownie, or bridging Brownie Girl Scouts. You will also learn more about the things you like to do, grow in leadership skills, and be a role model to younger Girl Scouts. Here are the requirements:

JUNIOR AIDE

1

Get Ready: Talk with your Girl Scout leader or the person who is helping you in Girl Scouting about becoming a Junior Aide. With her help or the help of your Girl Scout council, find a troop or group of younger Girl Scouts you can work with.

Signature:

What I did:

What I learned:

2

Get Set: Talk to the leader of the troop or group of younger Girl Scouts. Find out what you can do to help out. Arrange with the Daisy Girl Scout or Brownie Girl Scout leader the times, dates, and places that you will get together with the younger girls. Discuss with her the activities you would like to lead for at least three meetings. You can use the Action Plan in the "Adventures in Girl Scouting" chapter for help in planning.

Signature:

What I did:

What I learned:

3

Go! Meet with the younger girls. Partner with an adult leader to guide the activities you chose. Use the activity ideas below to help you plan:

- Teach the girls a Girl Scout game or song.
- Lead an activity for Daisy Girl Scouts to earn a petal or for Brownie Girl Scouts to earn a Brownie Girl Scout Try-It.
- Help Brownie Girl Scouts complete their bridging activities.
- Help younger girls complete a service project.
- Plan a meeting in which you introduce outdoor activities to guide girls as they explore their environment.
- Introduce girls to activities from *Girl Scouts Against Smoking*, an *Issues for Girl Scouts* book, or *GirlSports Basics*.
- Invite younger girls to participate in a Junior Girl Scout activity—at a troop meeting or on a trip.
- Work with younger girls at a council-sponsored event.
- Help girls plan a Thinking Day or other ceremony.
- Work with your adult partner to decide when you are finished and if you are ready for the Junior Aide Award. The leader of the younger girls and your Girl Scout leader will sign below:

Leader from troop I worked with:

My Girl Scout leader:

Junior Girl Scout Leadership Award

The Junior Girl Scout Leadership Award offers you an opportunity to develop your leadership skills as you give service to your Girl Scout troop/group and in the community. By completing the leadership activities in this award, you will uncover the leader within you! Complete Step One first and Steps Two and Three in any order; do Step Four last. Here are the requirements:

Date award completed:

Leader's signature:

1

Link to Leadership

Read the group and leadership sections in the "Adventures in Girl Scouting" chapter of this book. Decide what leadership qualities you would like to develop and write them here:

2

Succeed at Service

Develop leadership qualities by giving service to a community, school, religious, or Girl Scout organization. Your service experience must total at least six hours. Examples of community service opportunities are:

- Volunteering at an animal shelter or at the library
- Helping at a day care center
- Tutoring a younger child
- Working on a troop newsletter
- Reading to a person who is elderly or blind
- Being a coaching assistant for a sports team

My service experience involved:

3

Position Yourself

Develop leadership qualities by serving in a leadership position for at least one month. You may serve in a troop/group, school, club, community, or religious setting. Examples of leadership positions include:

- President
- Vice President
- Secretary/Recorder
- Treasurer
- Patrol Leader
- Assistant Patrol Leader
- Team Captain
- Assistant Captain
- Leader's or Teacher's Assistant

My leadership position was:

4

Mentor (Teach) Others

Help others gain from the things that you have learned. In your troop/group meeting share what you learned while completing Steps Two and Three. Explain how you served actively and responsibly in each step. Describe how the leadership experiences you completed helped you develop the qualities you listed in Step One.

Bridging to Cadette Girl Scouts

Moving from one Girl Scout level to another is called bridging. You can begin to bridge to Cadette Girl Scouts in your last year as a Junior Girl Scout. As a Cadette Girl Scout, you will enjoy many of the same types of activities you did in Junior Girl Scouting, but as a Cadette Girl Scout you have more freedom, greater opportunities, and more responsibilities.

What Is It Like to Be a Cadette Girl Scout?
As a Cadette Girl Scout you have the opportunity to do Interest Projects, go on longer trips, teach sports skills to young girls, and earn a Silver Award and other awards. When you are ready to take the following bridging steps, you can earn your Bridge to Cadette Girl Scouts Award. Here are the requirements:

1

Find out about Cadette Girl Scout books. Look through the *Cadette Girl Scout Handbook* or the *Interest Projects for Cadette and Senior Girl Scouts* and pick three activities that interest you.	1	2	3

2

Find out about GirlSports or other council-sponsored opportunities for Cadette Girl Scouts. Participate in one where Cadette Girl Scouts are also taking part. My experience involved:	

3

Do one of the activities you picked in Step One, which you didn't do yet.	

4

Participate in a service project with a Cadette Girl Scout. Or participate in a camping or hiking trip with a Cadette Girl Scout troop. My experience involved:	

5

Do something with a Cadette Girl Scout or Cadette Girl Scout troop. My experience involved:	

6

Help plan your bridging ceremony. Plan ways to make your ceremony meaningful and unique for you and other Junior Girl Scouts who are bridging with you.	Date completed:	Signature:	Leader's signature:

The Girl Scout Bronze Award

The Girl Scout Bronze Award is the highest award a Junior Girl Scout can earn. It shows you have made a promise to help others, improve your community and world, and become the best you can be.

The first three requirements of the award help you build skills and will prepare you for the fourth requirement, a Girl Scout Bronze Award Project. Work closely with your Girl Scout leader or Girl Scout advisor in completing these requirements.

Brownie and Junior Girl Scouts learn about environmental issues from a marine biologist.

How to Earn the Award

1. Decide on your Girl Scout Bronze Award service project. Read the requirements for the project to help you decide.
2. Do the first three requirements in any order, but they must be completed before you start your project. You may not use one activity to apply to more than one requirement.
3. You can work with other girls on the Girl Scout Bronze Award Project. If you and a group of girls decide to do the project together, each girl must be responsible for a part of the project. She must be able to show exactly what she did and what she accomplished.

Sample project

A Junior Girl Scout called the activity leader at a local nursing home and arranged to help residents plant a garden. She found out from the residents what they wanted to plant, helped them plant seeds and seedlings, and came by weekly to help them weed. When the garden was in bloom, she took photos and mounted a display in the nursing home's cafeteria.

Sample project

A group of Junior Girl Scouts worked with their Girl Scout council to improve their camp's meeting center. They painted a room at the center, collected books, games, and sports equipment, and set up a way to store these items.

Sample project

A group of Junior Girl Scouts created a sports day activity based on GirlSports and took it "on the road" to younger Girl Scout troops and groups in their community.

1

Earn two badges that are related to the project you will do for your Bronze Award. For example, if you choose a project that improves the environment, earn the "Eco-Action" and "Earth Connections" badges. If you are doing a project that helps senior citizens, you could earn "Across Generations" and "My Community."	Badge one:	Badge two:
	How these badges are related to my project:	
	Signature:	Leader's signature:

2

Complete one of the Girl Scout Signs (see details earlier in this chapter). The Girl Scout Signs are based on the four Girl Scout program goals for girls. You learn skills to become a successful and capable Junior Girl Scout when you complete a Sign.	Name of the Sign:	
	By doing this Sign, I learned that I can:	
	Signature:	Leader's signature:

3

Earn the Junior Aide Patch OR the Junior Girl Scout Leadership Award OR two of these badges: "Girl Scouting in the USA," "Girl Scouting Around the World," "Girl Scouting in My Future," and "Lead On."	What I did:	
	What I learned:	
	Signature:	Leader's signature:

4

Do a Girl Scout Bronze Award project. This project shows the leadership skills you have learned as a Junior Girl Scout, and your commitment to your community and to yourself. To earn this award, you will do a project that shows that you understand and live by the Girl Scout Promise and Law.

The project should:

- Take approximately 15 hours to complete (this includes planning time). Doing the project should take at least seven to eight hours.
- Provide community service, but can be done in or outside of Girl Scouting.
- Follow the Action Plan in the "Adventures in Girl Scouting" chapter of this book. This should be a new service project that you or you and your troop or group have decided to do to earn this award. It should not be something you have already done.
- Follow safety rules. Check with your leader or Girl Scout advisor about which safety rules apply to your project.

Index

a

b

c

Index

METRIC *Conversion*

CUSTOMARY TO METRIC

Customary		Metric
1 inch (in)	=	2.54 centimeters
1 foot (ft)	=	.3 meters
1 yard (yd)	=	.9 meters
1 mile (mi)	=	1.6 kilometers
1 acre	=	.4 hectares
1 quart (lq) (qt)	=	.9 liters
1 gallon (gal)	=	3.6 liters
1 ounce (avdp) (oz)	=	28.4 grams
1 pound (avdp) (lb)	=	.5 kilograms
1 horsepower (hp)	=	.7 kilowatts

UNITS OF LENGTH AND MEASURE

Length

12 inches	=	1 foot
36 inches or 3 feet	=	1 yard
1760 yards or 5280 feet	=	1 mile

Liquid Measure

8 ounces	=	1 cup
16 ounces or 2 cups	=	1 pint
32 ounces or 4 cups or 2 pints	=	1 quart
64 ounces or 4 pints or 2 quarts	=	1/2 gallon
128 ounces or 16 cups or 8 pints or 4 quarts	=	1 gallon

METRIC TO CUSTOMARY

Metric		Customary
1 centimeter (cm)	=	.39 inches
1 meter (m)	=	3.3 feet
1 meter (m)	=	1.1 yards
1 kilometer (km)	=	.6 miles
1 liter (l)	=	1.1 quarts (lq)
1 cubic meter (m3)	=	284.2 gallons
1 gram (g)	=	.04 ounces (avdp)
1 kilogram (kg)	=	2.2 pounds (avdp)
1 kilowatt (kW)	=	1.3 horsepower

TEMPERATURE CONVERSIONS

From Fahrenheit to Celsius

To convert from degrees Fahrenheit to degrees Celsius, subtract 32 degrees from the temperature and multiply by 5/9.

From Celsius to Fahrenheit

To convert from degrees Celsius to degrees Fahrenheit, multiply the temperature by 1.8 and add 32 degrees.